PASTA & PIZZA

Jaet Boilly d'après nature 1827.

46.

Lith. de Engelmann.

COSTUMES ITALIENS.

(Milanais.)

A Paris chez Daudet rue Marie Stuart N.º 8.

PASTA & PIZZA

Introduction by MASSIMO ALBERINI
Recipes compiled by ANNA MARTINI
Translated from the Italian by ELISABETH EVANS

ST. MARTIN'S PRESS NEW YORK

Martini, Anna.
    Pasta & pizza

                Translation of Pasta & pizza
1.   Cookery (Macaroni)   2.   Pizza.   I.   Alberini,
Massimo   II.   TITLE.
TX809.   M17M3713   641.6'31'1   76-50556

CONTENTS

130 NEW AND FANCIFUL PASTA RECIPES

PASTA

INTRODUCTION

During the last century so much was written about foreign travel that people acquired a new interest in how other nations lived. These accounts also inspired mental images of foreign eating habits. It was easy for the average reader to imagine the English living solely on a diet of roast beef, the Germans on sausages and potatoes and the French as the only people who would ever dream of eating frogs. Italians were always associated with pasta, and more particularly with macaroni.

The belief that macaroni was a uniquely Italian phenomenon stemmed from a general ignorance that pasta was also eaten in many other parts of the world. In this century, travel even further afield and better communications have shown that not just Italians, but also many oriental people, the Chinese and Japanese in particular, are great spaghetti eaters, although their pasta is not made from the same white flour as the Italians use. Prezzolini describes in his book *Macaroni & Co* how *tagliatelle* have been eaten in many parts of Europe from the earliest centuries, and were known by different names deriving from the Latin *nodellus* or "little knot", because of the way the pasta gets tangled up in knots on the plate; for example the quite un-Italian sounding *nouilles* from France, noodles from England and German *Nudeln*. Until quite recently these foreign noodles were served in a very different fashion from their Italian "relatives" from the Abruzzi or Emilia (where *maccheroni alla chitarra* or *sagnette* were more like *tagliatelle* than macaroni, and were eaten with meat as part of the main course, rather than as a starter like the delicious *coq au Riesling* from Alsace). Nowadays, even in Italy, meals more often consist of only one main dish, so the gap between Italian pasta-eating habits and those of her neighbours is rapidly closing; one Bolognese restaurant even lists fish kebabs served with *tagliatelle* on the menu.

Another general misconception about pasta is that spaghetti was invented in the little towns from Torre Annunziata to Gragnano on the coastal strip between Naples and Sorrento. One source of this error may have been certain nineteenth-century writers such as Alexandre Dumas *père*, who visited Naples in 1835 and described the customs and eating habits of its inhabitants in a long work entitled *Grand Dictionnaire de la Cuisine*, or Francesco de Bourcard who compiled a more serious and interesting anthology on the subject a little later. Alternatively, misconceptions

Le Marchand de Macaroni à Naples.

Spaghetti vendors and clients in Naples, from a nineteenth-century French print. (Bibliothèque Nationale, Paris)

about the origins of spaghetti may have arisen from the arrival of Garibaldi and the Thousand in southern Italy in 1860. Garibaldi's followers came mainly from areas where soup was served with rice, such as Bergamo and Piedmont. In fact it was only a short time before the arrival of Garibaldi in Naples that the local *lazzari*, or street urchins, began eating macaroni or other pasta on anything like a regular basis. Even then it was rarely cooked at home; books by Delbono and the more colourful evidence of nineteenth-century lithographs by Dural, Ferdinando Palizzi and Duclère, as well as many anonymous watercolours of the Neapolitan school, show that it was common practice to buy a portion of pasta ready-cooked and mixed with cheese or tomato sauce from the nearest inn. Even the poorest Neapolitan enjoyed the human contact to be found in an inn, as well as his plate of *vermicelli* (little worms) and tomato sauce, or just *lattanti* (grated *pecorino* cheese). In one of the many comedies at the San Carlino theatre, Pulcinella refuses to enlist as a sailor because "there are no inns at sea".

So the Piedmontese, Lombards and Venetians who marched with Garibaldi made their first acquaintance with *vermicelli* and tomatoes. The history of this period is one of civil war, but one happy chapter was written in the kitchen: spaghetti, or *vermicelli* as it was known in southern Italy, became the national dish, although it was a long time before any sort of general consensus about cooking methods was achieved. In the South pasta was preferred very firm *al dente*, or *verdi verdi* (very green), in the words of Ippolito Cavalcanti, Duke of Buonvicino, who wrote the most important work on nineteenth-century southern Italian cooking. But it was generally believed by the Neapolitans that throughout the Paduan plain spaghetti was given the "wall test" — you threw it at a wall and if it stuck it was well and truly done. Quite rightly, southern methods came to triumph in this field, just as pasta came to triumph over rice.

Two regions were unaffected by the encroachment of southern pasta traditions: Liguria and Emilia. In Liguria *lasagne* and *fidei* were part of the basic diet long before Garibaldi's Neapolitan adventure. The oldest document in Italian mentioning macaroni is part of an inventory drawn up by the notary Ugolino Scarpa, dated 2 February 1279, which lists among the possessions in the estate of Ponzio Bastone, soldier, a chest of macaroni. Emilia had long been the home of fresh *lasagne* and *tagliatelle*, and both these regions were to play a leading part in shaping the pattern of life in the newly unified state of Italy. The former Ligurian republic of San Giorgio contributed its own lenticular-shaped *trenette* to the national catalogue of flat pasta — the most confusing

Lectern, vase and Capodimonte figurine showing typical pasta-eating scenes. (Museo Agnesi Pontedassio, Imperia)

category of all, as nobody can ever agree about the correct appearance of any of the different varieties from *linguine* to *tagliarelli*. Bologna was also able to "export" its own egg pasta to other regions without any argument, even in parts where for reasons of economy pasta was thought of only in terms of a flour and water dough – cut off from the Kingdom of Sardinia in 1859, the county of Nice escaped the Emilian influence and to this day serves tourists and inhabitants alike with "real" ravioli made with the original flour and water dough.

There are many theories about the origins of pasta in Italy and in other parts of the world, but nothing is certain. The painted stucco reliefs in the Tomba dei Rilievi at Cerveteri (Caere) show domestic utensils including a table used to make the pasta dough, known as the *spianatora* (rolling-out table) in Roman dialect, a rolling-pin, knives and even a little indented pasta wheel which cut crinkly-edged *lasagne*, so the Etruscans obviously enjoyed home-made pasta. Excavations at Pompei have not yet revealed any evidence of pasta-making in Roman times, but according to Forcellini's *Lexicon*, and a passage in a book by Paolo Monelli, the word *lagana* or *lasagna* was in use at the time of Cicero.

In any case, the innumerable references to plates of pasta in manuscripts of all types (not merely those dealing with cooking), dating back to the thirteenth century, indicate that pasta spontaneously became a part of the Italian diet – like roasted or boiled meat, vegetable soup, flat bread – arising from the general populace itself, without any special suggestion or guidance from experts.

In the whole history of cooking there have been very few genuine inventions, and there is even doubt as to whether it was Louis Nointel de Béchamel, gentleman banker at the Court of Louis XIV, or his anonymous cook, who invented the famous white sauce known as *béchamel*.

The linguistic origin of *maccherone* (macaroni) has been long debated. It may derive from Macco, a character in Atellan farces, or from *macco*, a word still widely used in Sicilian cooking for a flour and water dough, or even from the Greek *makar*, meaning blessed, or food of the blessed. Paolo Monelli made an amusing and extensive investigation into the linguistic origins of macaroni in his preface to *230 Ways of Cooking Pasta* by the Jarratts, published in 1969. He also mentions the part Marco Polo was supposed to have played in all this. It appears that the only reason some Italians still believe Marco Polo first brought pasta to Italy from the East is because of an (unsigned) article that appeared in the October 1929 edition of the *Macaroni Journal*, an American trade journal of the pasta industry. Entitled "A Saga of Cathay", it tells how on his journey to China Marco Polo sent a sailor ashore in search of fresh water; this sailor reached a village where he saw a native and his lady making some strange food consisting of long strands which were cooked in boiling water. The sailor obtained the secret of this food and brought it back to the West; his name was none other than Spaghetti – perhaps the main reason for treating the whole story as somewhat less than the truth.

In fact Marco Polo does relate that in Fanfur (Sumatra?) he ate *lasagne* made from the flour of the bread fruit tree and that this flour was used "to make other things, just as we use wheat flour". The *Milione* was dictated by Marco Polo to Rustichello da Pisa in 1298, while it has been already mentioned that Scarpa, the notary in Genoa, wrote about the existence of macaroni in Italy twenty years earlier.

Pasta is well documented in poetry and literature, from Boccaccio's land of Bengodi to the *La Secchia Rapita* or *The Rape of the Bucket* by Tassoni (in Canto 4 Tassoni attributes the invention of *pappardelle* to a certain Baccarin da San Secondo, to whom a street in Modena was subsequently dedicated). There is also the burlesque *maccheronico* verse by Merlin Cocai, and a poem written in 1670 by Francesco De Lemene entitled *Discendenza e nobiltà dei maccheroni* (The Noble Lineage of Macaroni), which was warmly praised by Redi and by Ugo Foscolo himself. Italian poetry has tended to confuse the sublime with the ridiculous, especially when the subject is food, such as the various *Salameidi* (In Praise of Salami), or the *Elogio del Porco* (In Praise of the Pig). But the literary fortunes of spaghetti are due more to its unique appeal to the imagination; spaghetti is a zany food and any pasta, from *maltagliate* (badly cut) to *ziti*, has a funny shape that makes it difficult to eat, and thus a good subject of mirth, especially when a cunning photographer catches some glamorous star or politician rolling obstinate spaghetti round a fork.

Many ancient documents trace the early history of pasta in Italy, but among the strangest is the account of the beatification of Guglielmo Cuffitella, born in Sicli, Sicily in about 1351, who died in 1404 in the odour of sanctity and has since been known as William the Hermit. Documents included in the *Acta Sanctorum,* by the Jesuit fathers Bolland and Papebroch (volume IX, 1675) relate how Pope Paul III opened the process of beatification in 1537. A successful result to such a process would be highly unlikely today, but at the time of Paul III even the devil's advocate had to withdraw in the face of miraculous evidence concerning pasta.

Pinelli fece

2

Venditore di Maccaroni
in Napoli

There were three characters in the little drama: Blessed Guglielmo, his friend and companion Guiccione, and Guiccione's wife, a nasty spiteful piece of work if ever there was one.

First of all Guiccione invited Guglielmo to dinner and his wife made ravioli. She stuffed Guglielmo's portion with bran and other inedible things (a trick still played by some Italians, who give their friends ravioli filled with things like cork or bits of rubber as a joke). Guglielmo made no comment but blessed the ravioli. A miracle! At his request Guiccione and his nasty wife tasted the ravioli and they were full of ricotta, and thus Guglielmo was hailed as the inventor of *tortellini di magro*, or ravioli filled with cheese for the Lenten fast.

Next Guglielmo refused a second invitation to a meal, so Guiccione sent round a dish of nice hot *lasagne*. The day was Ash Wednesday; his wife made no objection but she secretly told the boy taking the *lasagne* to hide them in a cupboard in the Hermit's house and not to tell him anything. And so it happened. Lent went by and Guiccione began to wonder why Guglielmo had not sent back the *lasagne* dish. The boy was sent off to inquire about it. The Hermit pretended to be surprised, opened the cupboard and revealed the original plate of *lasagne* all piping hot as if it had just come out of the oven. So the nasty wife was confounded and the saint's virtue exalted.

In more recent times Gioacchino Rossini did wonders with pasta, even if he could not quite run to miracles. It was not so much when he was composing (in fact he wrote *Otello* in Naples as guest of the impresario Barbaja, who tried to goad him into doing some work with the threat that he would shut Rossini up "with just two plates of macaroni a day"), as when he was living a carefree life in Italy and Paris, well out of the musical rat-race. His luncheons and dinners in the Chaussé d'Antin were famous even in Paris of the 1860s, at a time when "la grande cuisine" flourished in private homes and restaurants, some of which carry on the same tradition today — the Grand Véfour restaurant in Paris, for example. Rossini had his pasta sent from Naples; a delightful letter on the subject survives dated 4 March 1859 and signed "Rossini senzamaccheroni" (macaroni-less Rossini). He then cooked it himself for a variety of guests including agents, singers and pianists.

His favourite recipe, called after him, is fairly complicated. He made a soft filling of truffles, *pâté de foie gras* and beef marrow and then injected it into a large type of macaroni, rather like *cannelloni*, with a silver and ivory syringe. But he did not only specialize in complicated dishes, as can be seen from the rules for serving real Italian pasta which he confided to his friend Jacopo

Scale model of a mule operating the pasta-making machinery in a nineteenth-century Ligurian pasta factory. (Museo Agnesi, Pontedassio, Imperia)

Caponi, and which are still quite valid today: "A dish of macaroni is only good if you use good pasta, the best butter and really excellent tomato sauce and parmesan. You need intelligence to cook, mix and serve pasta."

Gnocchi, lasagne and spaghetti

Pasta is such a natural food that it is quite easy to trace what De Lemene called "the noble lineage of macaroni" with the help of early manuscripts and a little imagination. Primitive man first discovered cereals in a wild form and cultivated them, so the early caveman chefs cooked with barley, oats, millet and many other grains that are no longer used, such as *spelt*, and this gradual development is still at work today. At first the grain was just roasted in the husk, then the husk was removed and the grain was boiled up whole (and there are still some barley soups made in the Trentino, or the Sicilian *cuccia* desserts, that derive from this early method). Finally it was discovered that by grinding and sieving the grain it was possible to obtain a powdery substance much easier to cook into a sort of thick porridge (*polenta*, which came from the Latin *puls*), or to make into fairly thin flat buns that were originally cooked on hot stones, like the *piada* from Romagna and *burgutta* from Eritrea still made today. The name of the primitive product of a millstone or pestle came from *farro*, or *spelt*; in Italian it became *farina* and in English, flour.

A major problem for any age has been to find ways of preserving fresh or leftover food as long as possible, or of disguising it in many different recipes to vary the taste and appearance. A huge step forward was made with the discovery of yeast as a leavening agent; this improved the taste, the nutritional value and also the keeping quality of bread and other flour-based products, but for many centuries peasant women faced the problem of making the bread to keep for several days. And then someone also thought of shaping the usual flour and water dough into little irregular balls and cooking them in boiling water.

So *gnocchi* were born. For over a century now, since the potato became supreme in the kitchen, *gnocchi* have been generally associated with a dough of puréed potato and just a little white flour, but originally they had to be made without the "wonderful fruit of America", as the potato has been described. The original flour and water recipe can be still seen in certain Sardinian *gnocchi* called *malloreddus*, and in the *knödeln* from the Alto Adige which are made just as they were in the Renaissance, with flour, breadcrumbs and often also liver, the local cured pork and plums.

Above left: apparatus for cutting penne, *from the long strands of macaroni that came from the extrusion press. A series of knives were set in the lid and when closed it cut the* penne *to the desired length.*
Above right: stone wheel used for kneading the flour and water dough. It then went into the press which had different dies to make the different sorts of pasta. (Museo Agnesi, Pontedassio, Imperia)

Gnocchi were sometimes known as macaroni, perhaps because the soft *gnocchi* dough resembled a bean *polenta* called *macco*. The illustrations to the sixteenth-century burlesque macaroni poem *Baldus* show the muses Togna and Zane eating forkfuls of *gnocchi* as big as fish cakes, so the mock Latin poetry of the author, Merlin Cocai (pen name only), should have been called *gnoccolare* instead of *maccheronico*. Since the inhabitants of Boccaccio's Bengodi rolled their macaroni down a mountain of parmesan ("They rolled them down and the more they rolled the more there were..."), they must have been round like *gnocchi*, not *penne*, *zite* or spaghetti. In addition the whole question of the original confusion between *gnocchi* and macaroni is clearly illustrated in the sixteenth-century cookbook *Banchetti*, by Cristoforo da Messisbugo, the carver and cook to the court of Cardinal Ippolito d'Este at Ferrara. Messisbugo gives wonderfully precise instructions for making macaroni from a dough made with eggs, for (as every housewife knows) they hold the dough together better in the boiling water. Then he goes on, "Cut the dough in pieces the size of a chestnut and shape them into macaroni by pressing them against the back of a grater" — which is exactly how *gnocchi* have always been made.

So even in the sixteenth century there was confusion about pasta terms: Messisbugo in fact calls *lasagne maccheroni alla napoletana* ("Cut the dough in long narrow strips"). In the Paduan plain macaroni is still synonymous with *gnocchi*, and the word also means a stupid person, easily duped.

It is more than likely that the rolled-out sheet of pasta dough evolved at about the same time as these lumps of dough that were used to make macaroni/*gnocchi*. This was obviously a spontaneous development in other parts of the world as well, including China and Japan; the flour and water dough was flattened by rolling it with something, then cut in pieces and cooked in water or stock while it was still fresh and soft, or after it had been left to dry outside in the sun.

It is interesting to see how from earliest times, or from the earliest records at least, people tried to make this pasta dough more interesting by inventing a variety of fillings to cook inside it. There may have been two reasons for this: the servants and lesser courtiers were perhaps given the remains of the great banquets, chopped up and used as a pasta filling (in Piedmont *agnolotti* are still made with cooked meat, and especially the braised meat and vegetables that have always been the standby of thrifty people). Alternatively, the stuffed pastas were sometimes a superior dish in their own right and the best ingredients were used for the fillings, such as the veal, pork, chicken and parmesan cheese that make the Bolognese and Modenese stuffed pastas so delicious and cause such argument between the two cities as to the relative superiority of their different recipes. There are also the cheese and vegetable pasta fillings, which in a way link the "leftover fillings" and the "treat fillings", as they were not born from any gastronomic necessity but as a result of the church fasts which dictated the family diet on Fridays, during Lent, on Ember Days, Vigils and the like for so many centuries, and which have now almost completely disappeared from the church calendar. Mantuan pumpkin-filled *tortellini* were created in response to fast day regulations, and also the rarer *sguazzarotti*, or *tortellini* filled with spinach or Swiss chard and ricotta, which were made in some form or other in nearly every part of northern Italy, without any acknowledgement to William the Hermit and his miraculous ravioli.

There is further evidence in an anonymous Tuscan manuscript in the University Library of Bologna (reprinted in Professor Faccioli's marvellous collection of early cookery manuscripts, *Arte della Cucina*). Professor Faccioli dates it to the early fifteenth century and it contains recipes for *lasagne* and *tortelli*, although the *tortelli* are cooked in a frying pan in oil and pork fat. However the *panzerotti* from southern Italy date from even earlier times.

The history of spaghetti, *vermicelli* and their like shows the development from fresh to dried pasta — it was originally more common to cook *lasagne* immediately instead of leaving them to dry — and also how pasta-making became an industry. The pasta industry was born from the discovery that hard wheat flour was superior to ordinary wheat flour for making pasta, as the dough did not fall apart in the boiling water, and also that the climate of certain parts of Italy was ideal for drying pasta as there were no sudden daytime variations in temperature and humidity. So pasta factories sprang up in coastal areas blessed with more sun than rain, with good land and sea breezes and no mist or fog. For centuries early cookery manuscripts and various edicts and proclamations mention Sicilian and Sardinian macaroni, pasta from Genoa (and only much later from Naples); the price was carefully regulated and its sale was limited in times of famine, so it was obviously very special. Three things ruined families, according to the *Pentamerone* written by G. B. Basile at the beginning of the seventeenth century: *zeppole* (fried pastries), white bread and macaroni.

Pasta continued to be made in the same simple way right up to 1939 when, after experimental periods in France under the guidance of the ex-brickmaker Sandragné and in Italy at the factories of the Braibanti company, a whole floor of the great Agnesi pasta factory at Imperia was equipped with a continuously operated mechanical press, capable of transforming flour and water into any sort of pasta imaginable in a continuous process. This method was then adopted throughout the industry.

Before 1939 the work of pasta-making had been organized in three stages. In the first stage the flour and water were mixed. Secondly, the dough was put in a kneader; in the South three or more men operated a sort of bar to rotate it, whereas in Liguria it was done with a wheel rotating in a wooden trough. When the dough was smooth and compact it went through a third stage, by which a mechanical press (*l'ingegno*, or "gadget", invented by the Neapolitans) with a screw plunger pressed the pasta down on to a perforated copper disc, the die-plate, which could be changed to make spaghetti, macaroni, *rigatoni* or other similar shapes, and a revolving knife then controlled the length of the pasta as it came through the die-plate (short pasta was made when the knife worked extra fast).

The pasta was next laid across canes hooked on to a wooden frame to dry. The frame was put out on a terrace or over the street in southern Italy, or propped up against more canes in a well ventilated room in Liguria.

Pasta-making was by no means easy; each stage required careful supervision, from the temperature of the water and the amount of kneading and pressing to the length of the drying period, which varied according to time, place and weather. There was much rivalry and intrigue about the carefully guarded secrets of manufacturing processes. To make or sell pasta it was necessary to belong to a guild, in accordance with the statute of the Arte dei Fidelari (Pasta-Makers Guild), laid down in Genoa in 1538. Various other exclusive academies and universities of *vermicelli*- and *lasagne*-makers exercised a rigid control over the whole industry. In the sixteenth century there were many famous disputes between the bakers and pasta-makers about who had the right to sell dried or fresh pasta in Rome.

Naples launched its own pasta industry on a national scale in the second half of the nineteenth century in the face of traditional opposition from the North, which firmly believed its own pasta to be better than anything produced along the coast south of Naples. Eventual Neapolitan ascendancy in the field was really a result more of technical advances than of climate. In a study that appeared in the trade tournal *Molini d'Italia*, Vincenzo Agnesi gave some interesting details about these advances. In 1878 Neapolitan millers began to use the *semolatrice*, an automatic sifter invented in Marseilles, which produced a far finer flour than the usual hand-operated sieve. The workers at Torre Annunziata rebelled against the new machines and broke up the mills, burning the "Marseilleise inventions" or "starvation machines" as they called them. The local militia was called out and at the ensuing trial fifty people were given sentences varying between two and six years.

In 1882 the English were responsible for a fundamental change in the Neapolitan pasta industry. The famous firm of Pattison & Co. which had owned an iron-foundry in Naples for many years produced new mechanical kneading, extruding and cutting equipment. Meanwhile cylindrical rollers had also been developed. Here there were workers who did not rebel, even if the new machinery did put some of them out of work, and twenty years later Naples got its just reward. An official of the pasta-makers' union, Oddino Morgari, has calculated that in Torre Annunziata alone about ten thousand people are employed in the pasta factories, in the port and other related industries, from the mechanics to the highly skilled wire-drawers who can perforate the bronze dies with over a hundred holes accurate to a tenth of a millimetre. The same is true at Torre del Greco, Gragnano, Portici and Castellammare. Pattison & Co. and their machines certainly contributed to the success of the Neapolitan pasta industry, and so of course did the Neapolitans, but some of the praise must still be due to Naples itself: *sarà l'acqua, sarà l'aria* (it could be the sea, it could be the air).

The Campania region also benefited enormously from Italian migration to the Americas. From the United States to the Rio del Plata, millions of good young Italians who worked so hard to make a living in Brooklyn or in the interior of Argentina asked little of their new country, but did insist on obtaining real Italian pasta. The Rubattino or Lloyd Sabaudo steamers that ferried to and fro across the Atlantic carried a cargo of Italian families, cases of *vermicelli* and barrels of tomato sauce and the best olive oil, all "made in Italy". This was the blue paper period: strong thick blue paper was used to line the crates that contained twenty-five or fifty kilograms of macaroni; it was used to wrap the long spaghetti in packs of two, three or five kilograms, sold under the Napoli Bella or Vesuvio brand labels. This thriving export industry was curtailed by such enterprising men as La Rosa, Caruso and Tampieri, who had sailed to America along with the pasta. Soon enough they realized that Canadian amber durum wheat was readily available to make pasta as good as any Italian variety. And it was their trade journal — or that of their descendants — that was responsible for spreading the story of Marco Polo and Spaghetti the sailor.

Naples was the centre of the Italian pasta industry for about half a century. The fame of its pasta is still undisputed but local producers have not really consolidated their achievement. There are too many small or medium-sized factories; nobody seems prepared to co-ordinate the industry or to organize the scattered units of production into a more coherent and efficient centre, or even to form a consortium to protect standards and copyright. Instead, northern industrialists have taken over the initiative. New techniques have made the industry less dependent on the vagaries of climate and season: special water treatment systems and drying rooms where temperature and humidity are carefully controlled have been developed so it is possible to create the ideal conditions for producing and drying pasta (the former is simpler than the latter). Naturally the industry developed best in areas where there was already an established tradition of pasta-making and where skilled craftsmen and a local market were immediately available.

Towards the end of the nineteenth century one of the leading Ligurian pasta-makers, Paolo Agnesi (the third generation in the business), went to the Campania with his technical manager to make an on-the-spot study of southern pasta-making techniques; he then set up first a section in his factory in Oneglia making Neapolitan-style pasta, then another making Genoese pasta, and another for Emilian *tagliatelle*. His sons and grandsons encouraged the transition from hydraulic presses to the continuous extrusion process and were the first pasta manufacturers to attempt modern methods of marketing their product. Pasta had never been really thought of under any specific brand names (in bakeries it was sold loose and you had to trust the baker as to its origin), so they began to use standard packs in clearly marked units of 200, 500 and 1000g. They also launched a modest sales drive aimed at informing the housewife about the advantages of durum wheat flour pasta, the evils of artificial colouring — it was quite legal then to use naphthol yellow to denote egg pasta — and about how to cook the pasta. Their efforts were rewarded and in 1939 Agnesi met their sales target of 2000 quintals (220·46 tons) output per day.

They were soon overtaken by other, older, established firms such as Buitoni from San Sepolcro and Barilla from Parma; Buitoni makes ordinary pasta and also dietetic products, while Barilla, which was founded in 1877 as an industrial bakery, set new records after the Second World War and has now reached its target output of 10,000 quintals (1107·30 tons) a day. Other well-known brands are from the North, such as Santi, Kim from Cremona and Arrighi, and the famous De Cecco brand from Fara San Martino in the Abruzzi in central Italy, but it is increasingly difficult to buy Neapolitan pasta.

The French, the Americans and even the Japanese are now making their own pasta, so the industry has become international and is no longer an Italian monopoly; nor is pasta such a uniquely Italian food.

Shapes, sizes and categories

Italian pasta is classified according to a great number of factors, but without going into too much detail here are the main categories.

The most important and ancient classification is according to the place of origin.

— *Pasta casalinga*, or home-made pasta, is prepared on the kitchen table (formica table-tops have almost completely replaced the wooden pasta board for this). It is made with very fine white flour — it takes the strong arms of a southern Italian housewife to make a durum wheat flour dough hold together — eggs and only rarely water.

The first step is always to put the flour in a mound on the table, then to make a well in it and break in the eggs. The ingredients are mixed in well to make a large ball which is then kneaded until it is firm and elastic. Following this, various procedures are used depending on personal and regional preferences. The traditional method which experts say is the best is to roll the dough out by hand. The rolled dough must be "light as a caress and round as the moon". The thickness will depend on what is being made, *lasagne* being thicker than *tagliatelle* for example, but above all the dough must be quite even and have no holes. At one time in Emilia and Romagna a girl who had holes in her pasta dough could never even dream of getting a husband. Then strips for *lasagne* may be cut with a knife or an indented pasta wheel, or the dough can be rolled up and cut in varying widths that have been calculated to the last millimetre for every sort of pasta. An Emilian proverb runs, "Short stories and long *tagliatelle*".

— Alternatively, the dough is put through the rollers of a little hand-operated machine which cuts it into the required widths. This is now the commonest method of rolling and cutting pasta used in Italy: the dough comes out more even and the strips are obviously a more regular width; however, the fastidious claim that the pasta loses some of its firmness and elasticity in the machine and that you can feel that it lacks "the loving touch of a woman's hand".

— Again, it may be put through a *torchietto* or pasta press. Once common, especially in the Veneto to make the whole wheat flour *bigoli*, served with sardine or duck sauce, it is now rarely used.

— *Pettine*, or combs, are curious instruments found in Romagna; the dough is cut in pieces and pressed against the comb to make a form of macaroni called *garganelli*.

— The *chitarra*, or guitar from the Abruzzi, has taut steel wires set at regular intervals in a rectangular wooden frame. The dough is rolled down on to the wires with a little rolling pin which cuts them into thin square strands, quite wrongly called *maccheroni (alla chitarra)*.

— The *ferro*, or needle, comes from Calabria, Apulia and Sicily as well as from other parts of southern Italy where it belongs to another tradition at least as old as *lasagne*. This involves quite a difficult operation: a small bit of dough is flattened out with the hand and smartly wrapped round the needle, which is either an ordinary knitting needle or a special square one, to produce a hollow piece of pasta about eight inches long. In some areas a willow twig is used instead of a needle as it is more supple and adaptable.

— *Ciurili* are used to make a small type of *gnocchi* called *malloreddus*, and so are not really eligible to be included in a list of pasta types, but since they are very popular and are made more than other potato *gnocchi* they are worth mentioning. The *ciurili* is a type of very fine wicker sieve which is used by Sardinian women to press or rub through the pieces of dough (made from durum wheat flour and water) and to give them their characteristic ridges. These sieves are an unusual and attractive shape and make one of the few authentic souvenirs possible to acquire in Sardinia.

— *Orecchiette* (little ears) (or *strascicati*, *strascinati*, etc.), the symbol of Basilican and Apulian cooking, are made without any special gadget other than a knife. You cut a little piece of pasta dough and press it with your thumb on a rough wooden surface to make a little shell.

— Other basic methods can produce *fusilli a ferro*, a type of macaroni — the dough is wrapped corkscrew-wise round a special needle-like instrument; the Genoese *corzetti*, obtained by cutting out the dough with a little mould (they were often decorated with attractive pictures — heads of Roman emperors, flowers etc.); and *passatelli* from Romagna, although this is not really pasta at all.

Usually home-made pasta is cooked and eaten as soon as it is made (in Milan there is a restaurant that specializes in cooking from the Abruzzi and the *maccheroni alla chitarra* is made while the customers are eating their first course). It is in fact fairly difficult to dry your own pasta and it is better to keep it in the refrigerator if you do not use it immediately.

Below left: Broad strips are cut from the rolled-up pasta dough in preparation for making pappardelle.
Below right: a torchio or hand press used in the Veneto for making bigoli *(thick whole-wheat spaghetti).*

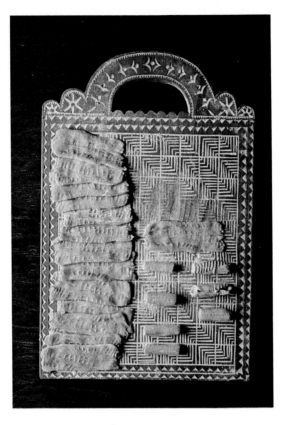

Above left: the chitarra *or guitar, a pasta-making instrument from the Abruzzi, consisting of a wooden frame with metal wires or "strings" set very close together. The rolled-out pasta dough is pressed down on the strings with a roller to make long square spaghetti called* maccheroni alla chitarra. *They are sprinkled with flour as they fall in the lower section so they do not stick together.*
Above right: an ancient board used for hand-pressed or -rolled forms of pasta.

Opposite: making testaroli *in Lunigiana. These flour and water pancakes are cooked in wide earthenware dishes called* testi. *The woman in this traditional kitchen is putting the lid on the dish which she will then cover with live embers and ashes. The pancakes are ready in about five minutes.*

Commercial pasta

The pasta industry produces dried pasta for the most part. By law this must be made only with pure durum wheat flour and water, without any artificial colouring or preservatives. It is permissible to add only natural ingredients such as green vegetables or tomatoes to colour the pasta, and they do not really alter the taste.

Egg pasta must contain at least five whole eggs for every 2lb flour. It is usually sold dried. Only a few delicatessens, shops and stores sell fresh egg pasta: it should be kept in a bowl or on a tray covered with transparent kitchen wrap in the refrigerator and cooked as soon as possible.

Two smaller and more recent by-products of the pasta industry are dried pasta-based soups (the packets contain everything for a *minestrone* or *consommé* with small pasta), and cooked pasta sold in tins.

Commercial pasta is almost always sold in standard packs: 200g, or $\frac{1}{2}$lb for small pasta (*pastina*) and 500g (or very rarely 1kg), or about 1lb (or 2lb) for other types. Dried pasta can keep for years in the right conditions. In 1946 a hotel in Aosta served spaghetti that had been hidden at the beginning of the war five years before. There is never any risk of pasta going mouldy in a clean house or shop.

The pasta industry has always had to face two problems: the availability of raw materials and the enormous variety of pasta types to be produced. Apulia, Sicily and Sardinia have never produced enough wheat for home consumption and it is thus necessary to import it. Formerly so much wheat was imported from South Russia that Genoese merchants had "trading posts" in the Crimea and along the Black Sea coast. The terrible famine of the 1918–19 civil war in Russia meant that durum wheat almost completely disappeared from the "lands of the black earth". Nowadays Canadian amber durum wheat, and wheat from the great reserves of the United States, is generally used instead.

The problem of pasta types was quite easily solved. Originally when the "pot" of the pasta press was empty the plunger had to be brought up again so more dough could be fed into the machine and the die plate at the bottom of the roller was quickly changed to produce, for example, spaghetti a few minutes after making *bucatini*. However nowadays any break in the production line is a waste of material and output. Besides, if there are too many types of pasta it creates problems for the packing machines. Formerly crates and chests were used for all types of pasta,

24

but now every variety has its own distinctive package designed to catch the housewife's eye in that vital split-second that is so finely calculated by market research teams.

So varieties of pasta have been reduced from 230–50 available in the last century to 50 or 60 presently on the market.

However, the traditional categories are still in common use.

Pasta lunga (long pasta). Originally about 1½ yards long, this was folded in half over a stick to dry, so it was about 2 ft when packed. Now it is cut into 8 in lengths and packed in boxes or bags.

The category of long pasta includes other types. There is round pasta without a hole. The thinnest sort is *capelli d'angelo* (angel hair), then *capellini* (little hairs, called *fidellini* in Liguria), and it gets gradually thicker with *vermicellini* (tiny worms), *vermicelli* (little worms), spaghetti, *spaghettoni*. The Ligurian varieties that were packed in a skein, such as *fidei* and *dapanieri* are now no longer found.

Round long pasta with a hole includes *bucatini, perciatelli, maccheroncelli, mezze ziti, zitoni* and *candele* (candles).

Square or convex long pasta includes *bavette, linguine* (little tongues), *lingue di passero* (sparrow tongues), *tagliarelli, tagliarellini* and *fettuccine lunghe*.

There is also frilly or curly-edged pasta: *ricciutelle* (curls), *reginette* (little queens) or *lasagne ricce*.

Pasta corta or short pasta. There are too many varieties of this to name them all. Different "groups" include round hollow pasta cut on a bias, such as *maltagliati, penne* (feathers), *mostaccioli, maccheroni, pennette* and *pennini* (pen points), all of which can be either smooth or ribbed. The most regular cylindrical pasta, which can also be smooth or ribbed, includes *ditali* (thimbles), *ditaloni* (big thimbles), *maniche* (sleeves), *mezze maniche* (short sleeves), *bombolotti, rigatoni, tortiglioni* and *cannelloni*. Then there are the shell types, such as *lumache* (snails), *lumaconi* (big snails), *conchiglie* (shells), *conchiglioni* (big shells), *gnocchi, abissini* etc. The *gomiti*, or elbow-shaped varieties (as they are known in the United States), include *chifferi, chifferotti, chifferoni* and *gramigna*. Finally there are the innumerable *fantasia* or "fancy" varieties that come and go on the market, such as *dischi volanti* (flying saucers) or *marziani* (Martians) according to fashion. In

Various types of commercial pasta: right, penne. *Opposite page: above left,* spaghetti; *above right,* lasagne *made with spinach purée; below left,* tagliatelle *"nests"; below right, grooved macaroni or* rigatoni.

Pasta manufacturers make special types of pasta to appeal to children, such as this dish of multicoloured tiny rings. The colours are made from natural ingredients such as spinach, beets, etc.

the last century there were even *assabesi*, named after the bay of Assab, the spearhead of the Italian colonies in Eritrea, and of course *garibaldini*.

Small pasta is divided into two sorts: tiny pasta for *consommé* and larger varieties for thick soups such as *minestrone*. Many of the original varieties have been abandoned, as they were considered old-fashioned, such as the highly imaginative *semi delle carte da gioco* (playing card suits), *minuscoli animali* (little animals), *mezzelune* (half-moons) etc. However there are still *pisellini* (little peas), *piselli* (peas) (*bombonin* in Piedmont), *puntine, puntette, semi di melone* (melon seeds), *risone, stelline* (little stars), *stellette* (pretty stars), *anellini* (little rings), *anelli* (rings), *quadrucci* (little squares) (usually only as egg pasta) and various sizes of *farfalli* (butterflies or bow ties). For vegetable-based soups there are *avemarie* and *paternostri* (named after the beads on a rosary), smooth or ribbed *ditalini, conchigliette, chifferini*, etc.

Egg pasta. This is also factory-made, using durum wheat flour, and then rolled out and cut according to Emilian types of pasta – the *tagliatelle, tagliatelle mezzane, tagliatelle larghe* or according to types from central and southern Italy such as *tagliolini, pappardelle, fettuccine* and the *lasagne* which are known all over Italy in varying widths, and which are packed in skeins or *nidi* (nests); alternatively the strips of pasta are pinched in the middle to make *farfalle, farfalloni, sorprese* (surprises), *margherite* (daisies), etc.

The lack of any really rational categories for pasta types complicates the pasta industry enormously, and manufacturers often use the same traditional names for very different sorts of pasta.

Spaghetti is a case in point. According to the manufacturer, this variety that has come to symbolize the whole of Italian cooking can be cooked in anything from six to fourteen minutes because it can vary so much in thickness (the strength and weakness of pasta is that the slightest change in thickness alters the taste completely); although fortunately it is universally accepted that it should be a long pasta without a hole. There are also other types like *maccheroni* (macaroni to the English-speaking world), which are sometimes known as *penne* in suppliers' lists, or relations of *zite* such as the *maccheroni di zita*, the bride's macaroni. For many centuries the Ligurians have never been able to agree about the exact shape and width of their *trenette*, and then there are the famous *maccheroni alla chitarra* which are really square *tagliatelle*.

It would in fact be excellent publicity for the pasta industry if all the manufacturers were to get together to draw up an approved catalogue of pasta types, and yet so far it has never been attempted.

Something has in fact been achieved, although in a rather more academic than practical way typical of such events, by the Bologna section of the Accademia Italiana della Cucina. Founded in 1953 by the journalist and author Orio Vergani and a group of well-known Milanese, including Arnoldo Mondadori the publisher, the "Accademia" has set itself the task of carrying out research into typical Italian dishes and of publicizing the restaurants that specialize in really good Italian cooking. Furthermore it holds study sessions attended by some of the 2800 members from 84 sections all over Italy to examine the economico-historical origins of Italian cooking and to try and establish some of the reasons why certain foods come and go in popularity and use over the centuries.

On 16 April 1972 the Bologna section of the "Accademia" met to present the President of the Chamber of Commerce with a little case containing the "golden rule of *tagliatelle*", or a solid gold *tagliatella* (noodle) of the ideal width, a standard established after extensive trials in the kitchen, to $\frac{3}{8}$in, or 1/12,270 of the height of the Torre degli Asinelli in Bologna (a perhaps over-academic distinction). Obviously it is not known whether Bolognese housewives and *sfogline* – the expert pasta-makers from Emilian inns of the past and present – will follow this golden measure slavishly. However, it is encouraging to see signs of interest in that people are thinking of pasta in terms of generally accepted classifications at all.

How to cook pasta

Southern Italy has gained advantage over the North by its adherence to the genuine rules of pasta cooking, so long forgotten or ignored in the plain of the Po.

The error of these northern ways spread to Germany, Switzerland and the parts of France where pasta is not part of any local cooking (in Alsace the *nouilles* that traditionally accompany *coq au Riesling* are always perfectly cooked), and where macaroni and spaghetti are more often than not overcooked to the extent that they end up a soft and soggy mess. It is almost as if the further north you go the more you must eat soft food that requires the least effort to chew, like velvety cream soups and semolina *polenta*. Until the return of Garibaldi's men from Naples good pasta was ruined by thirty or forty minutes in boiling water in households from Piedmont to the Veneto. People were convinced that overcooked pasta was more digestible, so they persisted in their error until dieticians revealed that pasta cooked *al dente*, or firm to the bite, needs chewing, and reaches the stomach in small pieces, which helps the gastric juices and ptyalin in the saliva, while on the other hand mushy spaghetti slithers unchewed into the stomach as a solid mass, putting a damaging strain on the whole system.

Another mistake made by northerners was to cook pasta in too little water. It was believed that you could cook 1lb pasta in about 2 pints of water. In fact, the cold mass of pasta plunged in insufficient liquid prevents the water from returning to a boil quickly, and when it does eventually boil the lack of water constricts the pasta and prevents some parts from absorbing any liquid at all. Durum wheat pasta absorbs an enormous amount of water, and many types, especially short varieties such as *farfalline*, treble or nearly quadruple in size as they absorb water. So too little water in the pan will produce nasty, sticky pasta.

Pasta manufacturers have been giving plenty of helpful publicity about how to cook their product for years now, so there should be few people who do not know how to set about it. Here are some very simple rules:

— Use 4 quarts of water to every 1lb pasta.
— Add salt when the water comes to a boil.
— Add the pasta all at once when the water is at a rolling boil and push it down immediately with a fork, stirring a little so nothing sticks to the bottom. (Be especially careful when adding nests or skeins of pasta and unravel them gradually with a fork; this applies also to flat varieties such as *lasagne* and *trenette* that tend to stick together.)
— Turn up the heat immediately to bring the water back to a boil. (You can cover the pan for a few

For successful pasta there are a few simple rules: use 4 quarts water to every 1lb pasta; add the salt when the water comes to a boil, then put in the pasta all at once and spread it out in the water (see opposite page, left); drain with a large fork, shaking the water off the pasta (right).

seconds, but remember that Dionigi Papin hailed the steam engine as a saucepan that did not need a lid, so make sure the water never goes off the boil.)

— Watch the pasta as it cooks. In spite of what the package says there is no precise cooking time for pasta. The same variety and brand can differ from one packet to another. This may be due to a corroded die plate on the extrusion press, or to the air, or to the interaction of water and air, or to the fact that the amount of water has not been accurately measured, or even to the altitude — at 2000 feet water boils below 212°F and the pasta is never so good. So keep looking at the pasta — or rather keep tasting it, as there are few cooks who can tell when it is really cooked from its appearance. The important thing is not to go away. An intelligent British writer put it in a nutshell: "Spaghetti likes company, don't leave it alone."

There was once a joke about sticky pasta for sticking posters, but the habit of overcooking it has been fairly generally rejected now. However, there is also the proverb, *Chi la vuol cotta, chi la vuol cruda* (Some like it well cooked, some like it raw), and tastes vary in this as in everything.

In fact, tastes vary from one region to another: in Naples chewy spaghetti is preferred (or *verdi verdi*, very green, in the words of the Duke of Buonvicino), with a soft outside and almost raw inner core. By Rome the cooking time is already longer; pasta is eaten *al dente* — a famous expression known all over the world which means that it is firm to the bite without being at all sticky or mushy.

Draining can make or ruin pasta, however perfectly you have cooked it. It should be done quickly (and the pasta should never stay in the cooking water after it is off the heat), but not too thoroughly. The trick of stopping the water boiling by adding cold water when you take the pan off the heat is quite a good one, but it is not essential, and has gone out of fashion now. There are various ways of draining the pasta, and the colander that is so universally used is probably the worst. It is infinitely preferable to follow the expert southern method of fishing the pasta out of the water with a fork, letting it drip a little, then transferring it at once to piping hot plates. The pasta will still be absorbing water so it will deal with any extra left on it in the few seconds before it reaches the plate and gets "sauced". However, few people use this method, and the old slotted flat ladles or spoons and the "*lasagne* box" of Liguria have almost disappeared. Gone too are the traditional and highly efficient little wicker baskets from Umbria which were used to fish out the pasta from the water, although they can still occasionally be found on stalls at country fairs.

Once the pasta is well drained it must be *condita*, or "sauced". Every part of Italy, often every single village, has its own sauce, which is considered vastly superior to any other. More is said on the subject in the next section, but here are some basic rules: mix the sauce and the pasta in a hot serving dish, using only half (or rather less if it has pieces of, say, meat or mushrooms in it), so that it mixes well and the pasta keeps its own shape rather than looking like a mound of sauce, then hand out piping hot plates and let everyone serve himself from the dish, and pass round the remaining sauce together with grated cheese.

There are no valid alternatives to these basic rules today. During the two world wars a special "cooking chest" was used to save fuel. It was lined with a heat-retaining material such as fibreglass (in the most expensive models) or woodshavings, and when the pasta had boiled for two minutes you took the pan from the heat and inserted it into the box. The temperature of the water slowly dropped from about 194°F to 158°F and the pasta cooked quite well; the larger varieties in particular did not break up, as they often tend to do. However, these chests are no longer available in the shops.

Some clever cooks manage to cook their pasta — especially the thick-leaf varieties, from *bombolotti* to *tortiglioni* — in a pressure cooker. But this is very tricky: one second too long and the pasta completely disintegrates and becomes quite inedible.

Recently some Emilian recipes have given instructions for stewing large varieties of pasta in the Bolognese sauce, or in any other thick, rich sauce in a pan without a cover for a few minutes before serving. But this again quite easily produces a mushy pasta resembling the worst of snack-bar food.

And after following the rules set out above you can just sit down and eat the pasta God has provided, in the words of Peppino De Filippo.

Regional recipes

Modern cooking trends have made pasta into a rich and over-substantial dish which takes on a more important role than it did traditionally and is eaten as a main course. This is of course far from the authentic recipes of Italian regional cooking. There are many such regional recipes in the first part of this pasta anthology, but here are some general points about Italian pasta.

First of all, it should be remembered that macaroni and *lasagne* started life, and this is confirmed by old cookery books such as Scappi, Messisbugo and Frugoli, as a middle course, or *piatto di mezzo*, to be served between the meat, fish and vegetable dishes that made up the *piatti di cucina* or hot dishes (the cold dishes were part of the *piatti di credenza*, or buffet course). The habit of serving pasta as a special first course came much later in both poor and wealthy households.

Secondly it should be remembered that pasta was originally served just with butter and cheese, plus the whole range of flavourings used in such abundance in Renaissance cooking, such as spices, sugar and often rosewater, and was then often baked in the oven or toasted on both sides to make a sort of pasta *au gratin*. Lasagne and macaroni were cooked in a fat stock and drained, then put in layers in a dish with grated cheese and butter and the usual spices. These old recipes can be modified to be less heavy and they still taste very good indeed. In fact the medieval preference for sweet and savoury mixtures is still common in certain parts of Italy, such as the Mantuan speciality, *tortelli di zucca*, or pumpkin-stuffed *tortelli*, which are served with *amaretti*, or little sugary almond biscuits, and the *gnocchi* served in the Veneto with butter, cheese and cinnamon. Some Sicilian pasta dishes include pine nuts, raisins and sugar (which also appear in the famous Sicilian recipe for pasta with sardines).

At the beginning of the nineteenth century macaroni served with just butter and cheese was considered to be the most traditional and acceptable style. In 1814 Vincenzo Agnoletti published his *Nuovissima Cucina Economica* in Rome, and it was so successful that a few years later he moved to Parma as cook, pastry-cook and distiller to Queen Marie-Louise. According to Agnolotti, *maccheroni alla napoletana* was a dish consisting of layers of macaroni, sliced *cacciocavallo* cheese, butter, grated parmesan and a little meat gravy baked in the oven until brown. The future chef to the unfaithful wife of Napoleon Bonaparte told how to make at least four types of tomato sauce, from a bottled variety to "bricks" of concentrated tomato dried out on the stove. At the same period another famous volume, *Il Cuoco Piemontese Perfezionato a Parigi*, gives a recipe for thick tomato soup, which in fact consists of rice with tomatoes, while pasta is to be served just with butter and cheese *al bianco*; and the author recommends *vermicelli* from Rivoli, a little village just outside Turin.

The first definite recipe for *vermicelli* with tomato sauce (*vermicelli co lo pommodoro*) appears in Ippolito Cavalcanti, Duke of Buonvicino's *Cucina teorico pratica con corrispondente riposto* in the 1839 edition, which is certainly the first book of its sort. For two *rotoli* (this Neapolitan measure was almost 2 lb) of *vermicelli* the Duke indicates four *rotoli* (about 8 lb) of tomatoes. They were to be cut in quarters, the seeds and water squeezed out and then they were boiled without any other ingredients, put through a sieve, reduced over heat and mixed with about $1\frac{1}{2}$ lb pork fat and stirred into the hot *vermicelli* with some salt and pepper. So the tomatoes were just "stewed" and served as they were. The Duke does not recommend cheese in this version, but he does for *maccheroni con la provola* (macaroni with *provolone* cheese), and for his macaroni with *brodo rosso dello stufato* (the red sauce from the *stufato*, the famous Neapolitan Sunday braised beef). He makes two further points of interest: the macaroni can also be served with fish stock or with cheese and beaten eggs – the former being an early version of *vermicelli alla marinara* and other seafood recipes, and the latter a version of *vermicelli alla carbonara*. *Vongole* (baby clams) are also suggested as an accompaniment to homemade *tagliatelle*.

Examination of more recent regional recipes that are still usable (the Duke's tomato sauce wouldn't appeal to many people now) confirms what is also a fact about rice recipes, and which upsets the traditional belief that northern cooking was superior to that of the South. The regions of Italy where less pasta was eaten in the late-nineteenth century were the ones to invent the most original and tasty ways of serving it. The South came to surpass the risotto of Piedmont and the Veneto with its own delicious *supplì, arancine* and *timballi*, reaching a peak of gastronomic extravagance with the Neapolitan *sartú di riso*.

Regional preferences are very obvious in these recipes. *Lasagne* and *trenette* were a very ancient and fundamental part of the cooking of Liguria centuries before Neapolitan pasta influenced the rest of Italy, while its sauces are mainly based on herbs (basil and wild marjoram), mushrooms, walnuts and less often chopped veal, sometimes with udders and sweetbreads. In Piedmont pasta consists mainly of *tagliatelline* – *tajarin* in the local dialect – mixed with chicken livers and truffles. Its fondue recipe is very good but is a completely modern invention.) Alba makes its own rather bizarre contribution to pasta cooking which is not even acceptable in other parts of Piedmont: *lasagne* with blood. The hot *lasagne* are fried in plenty of pig's blood together with sausage meat and pig's glands. There is only one really authentic dish from Lombardy: the *pizzocheri* of the Valtellina, which are home-made cakes of corn meal (maize flour or *polenta*) cooked in water with potatoes and vegetables, then drained and served with butter.

Bigoli, or thick whole wheat spaghetti, were the main speciality of the Veneto before it became subject to "foreign" influences. They were made by putting the pasta dough through a special hand press and were served with *salsa*, the word reserved in Italian for the famous Paduan speciality *bagna caôda*, also made in Mantua and Lombardy, consisting of anchovies and oil. They also come with chopped chicken or duck in a sauce. From the southern reaches of the Lombard league came *tagliatelle* – known as *paparele* in the parish of San Zeno – cooked in stock if they are fresh, or served with chicken livers if not.

We have no space to discuss the great pasta dishes of Emilia and Romagna at length, but the best are *tagliatelle* with Bolognese sauce, ham or fresh Italian sausage, and *lasagne*, which are either white or green, or used in alternate layers of both colours with *béchamel* and *ragù*, heated up in the oven without letting them brown. Emilia is considered to be the leading region for fresh pasta, but its stuffed pasta, especially *tortellini*, is justly famous. In spite of Boccaccio's ravioli the area where stuffed pasta, from *agnolotti* to ravioli and from *tortelli* to *cappelletti*, is made is limited to the region north of Rimini, across the Apennines to Modena where it links up with the ravioli area around La Spezia. Below this line stuffed pasta is less common and appears more often in cellophane bags of dried pasta than freshly made.

There is a less famous tradition which is equally typical of Emilia and Romagna and which has never caught on in surrounding regions: the fresh *garganelli* formed by pressing twists of dough against combs, and the *strichetti*, *maccheroncini* and *gramigna*. Nor must one forget one of the few remaining dishes to survive from the great Renaissance courts of the Este at Ferrara, and of the Gonzaga at Mantua, or of the Popes, since it is also a Roman speciality: the famous macaroni pie with its sweet shortcrust (*pasta frolla*) pastry case and pigeon sauce (and it does not include tomato since nobody had ever heard of a *pomo d'amore* in Italy when Cristofero da Messisbugo organized the banquets of Cardinal Ippolito d'Este).

Tuscany, Umbria and the Marches are a fairly unified area in cooking as in other things, so *pappardelle* with hare, duck and the black truffle of Norcia, or the local variety of baked pasta – the Florentine *lasagne alla fornaia*, and the *vincisgrassi* from the Marches (its strange name has never been properly deciphered) – are to be found in nearly every part.

Maccheroni alla chitarra, *orecchiette* and *vermicelli* are probably the most authentically traditional pasta dishes of central and southern Italy. Sicily needs excusing for one aspect of its cooking now, for although it has been influenced by four separate traditions – Greek, Arab, Norman and French – and is the richest in Italy, it is almost impossible to get to know its delights. From Catania, Palermo and Messina to all the smaller towns, nobody bothers to use more than a handful of well-known recipes, mainly the famous pasta with sardines, and other quick and easy dishes such as *tortellini alla bolognese*, which do not belong to the Sicilian tradition at all. Authentic Sicilian delicacies vary from the wonderful combination of pasta and eggplants (aubergines), such as *spaghetti alla Norma*, or *con le quaglie* (which in this case are not really quails, but fried eggplants (aubergines), *alla siracusana*, etc.; or pasta and broccoli *arriminati*, pasta and cauliflower, zucchini (courgettes), raisins and breadcrumbs with garlic, and so on from the simplest dishes to enormously rich and tasty concoctions such as *pasta incacciata*, *bomba di maccheroni* and *trionfo alla marescialla*. They are part of the tradition of family cooking, or "monzu's recipes", as French chefs were known in the Kingdom of the Two Sicilies (monzu = monsieur), and they are sadly lacking from Sicilian menus today. Strangely, the people most active in reviving this old cooking tradition are two Sicilian restaurant owners in Milan, Emanuele and Mimmo Brucia, both tremendous characters who are doing very well indeed.

Novelty is not always a good thing

This rapid survey of regional cooking in Italy shows the origins and development of the national dish. Today pasta cooking is in a somewhat different situation. The housewife and the chefs in both large and small restaurants are so pressed for time that they either adapt classical recipes (such as the many quick tomato sauces that have evolved over the years in every Italian home, or the simplified Ligurian *pesto* now made in the blender instead of pounding the oil and basil in a mortar, not to mention Bolognese sauce from a tin, or made with leftovers from the roast), or else they concoct their own special recipes which have no regional connections at all but are easily digested and please a demanding family. These include *tagliatelle* with butter and cream; pasta either with an authentic *sugo di carne* (meat gravy) or made from a bouillon cube and some butter; pasta with raw *ricotta* cheese (in fact an old Neapolitan dish); or pasta with tuna fish, diced *mozzarella* or processed cheese, frozen peas, butter heated with a few sage leaves, anchovy butter or even, although this is far less acceptable, with mayonnaise out of a jar. A true gastronome would deplore these modern trends, but everybody enjoys this sort of food, and that is the most important thing in cooking.

Traditional implements for draining pasta. (Museo Agnesi, Pontedassio, Imperia)

However, this is not the case when it comes to some of the inventions, or "secrets" as they like to call them, of the hotel and restaurant trade.

One recipe in particular has blinded people to the genuine rules of good Italian cooking. It was popularized by Roman restaurants just after the war, in about 1947, and then spread all over Italy: the recipe in question is *spaghetti alla carbonara*. The worst of postwar austerity was over, although food supplies were still irregular and rationing persisted, with its concomitant black market. In Rome pasta-makers cooked and sold their wares in Piazza Vittorio just as in a nineteenth-century Dura lithograph. You went to a *trattoria* – the Re degli Amici was the most popular at the time – not to eat well but to eat a lot. *Spaghetti alla carbonara* became popular for this reason; it was a good substantial dish. I have already mentioned that this gastronomic absurdity must be attributed to a Neapolitan recipe, *maccaruni col caso e le uova sbattute* (macaroni with cheese and beaten eggs), if we are to accept the Duke of Buonvicino as a thoroughly reliable source. However, apart from mentioning it he gives no detailed recipe, and *spaghetti alla carbonara* does not appear in Artusi or in any other later cookbooks, not even in the *Cucchiaio d'Argento* published in 1950.

I personally believe that *spaghetti alla carbonara* was an emergency invention made by the American army of occupation in Italy. It was common for GIs on leave to go to little restaurants with their daily rations and ask the cook to make a spaghetti dish out of them. One cook probably saw the bacon and eggs and decided to mix the hot pasta with the fried bacon and the raw eggs in a very hot bowl so the eggs scrambled a little, and then he added a little grated cheese.

Whatever the story, the fact remains that *spaghetti alla carbonara* is a solid, filling dish that is no credit at all to real Italian cooking. The pasta is slimy rather than well covered in "sauce" and slippery, as it should always be. However, it has become an unbelievably famous dish, like other totally unauthentic creations such as *cannelloni alla Nizzarda* (quite unknown in Nice), and *maccheroni ai quattro formaggi* (and you are lucky if it really is made with four cheeses). Perhaps unintentionally, Italians have begun to follow the advice of the *Macaroni Journal*, which for years told Americans to "eat American spaghetti with American recipes", and to use less pasta and more and more sauces and relishes so they ended up with the dreadful spaghetti with meatballs that the Italians find so totally unacceptable.

Few restaurants are conscientious about using authentic recipes; instead, there is a tendency to invent pasta dishes so overloaded with ingredients that the bill is double or treble what it should be for a good honest plate of spaghetti with tomato sauce and butter. The customer is just as much to blame: people go to restaurants to eat a lot and to eat something other than what they eat at home. Little imagination goes into these extravagant creations; in fact, most effort is expended on finding a respectable or lewd name for the dish to amuse Italians and, as tourism increases, to entertain the more gullible foreigners who thought that *la dolce vita romana* began with *spaghetti alla puttanesca* (harlot's spaghetti). In spite of many different names the ingredients are always the same: chopped ham or bacon, sweet pepper, tuna fish, anchovies, mushrooms, shrimp or prawns, shellfish, garlic (to give an "authentic" flavour), onions, canned (tinned) peas and *pecorino* cheese, as well as the indispensable trio of Worcestershire sauce, cream and brandy – usually all just thrown together at random.

It is impossible to classify this sort of cooking. The most common names are, according to individual preference, *spaghetti alla boscaiola* (mushrooms and garlic), *alla bucaniera* (shrimp, meatballs, tomato and garlic), *alla Turiddu* (anchovies and olives), *alla tutto mare* (squid, shrimp, white wine, tomato), *alla marinara* (garlic, oregano), *alla trasteverina* (anchovy, tuna, tomato) and so on including the twenty-nine dishes which the actor Fabrizzi gives in his collection of poetry dedicated to pasta, such as *all'arrabbiata, alla cinese, alla tettatè, alla ladresca, alla carabiniera, alla papalina, alla scarpara, alla romanella, alla cacciatrice, all'acquamarina, alla scapola, al biondo Tevere, alla garibaldina, alla giudia, alla Trilussa*. Any one can make his own macaroni and call it *alla modo mio* and in fact Italians have to admit that foreigners such as Enrica and Vernon Jarratt are probably right when, in the preface to their book on pasta, they claim that pasta is just a vehicle for combining the most unusual variety of flavours possible. However, all these pasta dishes now exist, and if you write a pasta cookbook you must include them.

This culinary scandal is aggravated by the fact that in restaurants it has become common for perfectly cooked pasta to be heated up over a burner at the table. Smarter restaurants do this because the head waiter likes to take credit for the dish and enjoys the whole procedure. This large spirit burner in solid silver is wheeled in on a trolley by the head waiter followed by two assistants bearing the pasta on a silver serving dish, and whatever else is needed – a silver jug of cream, the sauce, cheese, brandy or whatever in a special bottle basket and a giant pepper grinder as big as a skittle. The show begins; moving with elegance and skill the head waiter mixes, pours, manoeuvres to heat up the dish of spaghetti, then melts the butter and pours in the cream to stop it sizzling, then adds the sauce to colour it and the cheese to turn it into an even stickier mess. The flaming brandy lit with an agile twist of the pan is the crowning glory of the whole operation and the diners approve it all with nods and smiles, ignoring the gusts of hot air and fumes from the burner. With the agility of a flamenco dancer the head waiter personally serves the prettiest girl with the first helping, and then abandons the rest to his assistants.

People who know and love pasta, the sort of people who drain it with a fork and not a colander, abhor this elaborate ritual. The pasta ends up all soft and greasy as the chef has already mixed it with butter in the kitchen so it is easier to handle, and then it is covered with far too much sauce heated up at the last minute, so the whole dish resembles a hasty preparation for late-comers rather than a fine example of Italian cooking. It has lost all that wonderful elasticity which should give a perfect bite to spaghetti (so the *spaghetti comminciono a ragionar col dente*, or begins to argue with the teeth), and affronts the natural affinity of wheat flour, butter and tomatoes. It is no more than a sticky mass of long gluey strands, hopelessly soggy on the outside and without any firm inner core.

Nevertheless, the head waiters will not give up this sort of practice and seem to enjoy their burners too much to do away with them (out they come again for that overrated and dubious dessert, *Crêpes Suzette*). Three years ago in the catering school of Bellagio a competition was organized for the best spaghetti. The first entrant prepared his offering over the burner; so did the second and the third. At that point the jury stood up and protested that so far nobody had received any points at all as their dishes showed all the worst defects in pasta cooking for Italians and foreigners to see. After that we succeeded in tasting twelve more very good dishes made as pasta should be made — without a burner.

Pasta abroad

A new international cuisine has been born from mass tourism and package holidays without anyone really noticing it. So far there has been no Escoffier to expound its theory and practice, but it is generally recognized by its average or below-average standards and achievement. The true gourmet who is ready to spend a little extra can still find genuine national cooking in every country, but if you arrive on a coach tour run along the lines of "if it's Thursday it must be Copenhagen" there is going to be little gastronomic variety. Everywhere convoys of tourists meet the same tomato salads and *crudités*, the same hamburgers (known in Italian as *svizzere*), which alternate with rather indistinguishable pieces of frozen fish, chops, *wienerschnitzel* and watery vegetable soups, and for supper the highly economical Spanish omelettes.

Spaghetti and pizza often figure on these sorts of menus. It is as well to forget that this is the Italian contribution to world cooking, but the matter is important enough to be discussed at length.

For the French, macaroni is an Italian dish but *tagliatelle*, or *nouilles*, are part of Alsatian cooking: the dough is made from 8 oz flour, 1 whole egg, 1 egg yolk and enough melted butter to bind. These noodles are three-quarters cooked in boiling water and then baked in the oven and served with butter in the same dish. This baking, we are assured by the monumental *Art Culinaire Français*, gives the dish a nice crispy top.

In 1846 Elmé Francatelli, a disciple of Carême, was chef at the court of St James and published an important collection of 1462 recipes called *The Modern Cook*. It does mention *maccheroni à l'italienne*, but *tagliatelle* are given as *à l'allemande* with a sweet sauce of cream, vanilla and almonds — not at all as it is made in Germany. But of course in West Africa *capelli d'angelo* are mixed with honey in a sort of pudding, then baked in the oven and not boiled (and here one could mention the Arab *trii*, which gave birth to the Sicilian pasta industry). There is a Greek cookbook by two ladies, Ms Vernos and Ms Prichard, with recipes in which pasta is included as an accompaniment to other things (and remember that non-Italian cookbooks used to put pasta with the vegetables), although this does not seem very genuine Greek cooking. You often see *Youverlakia me spaghetti* (spaghetti with meatballs) on Greek menus.

The Far East has a very different tradition. Myra Waldo, one of the most experienced American cooks in international cuisine, says quite rightly that in China rice and *vermicelli* are the basis of many dishes. People who like Chinese restaurants, if not in Canton, at least in Amsterdam (which has the largest number of restaurants serving oriental food per head of population), London or Paris will agree. It takes no great knowledge of Chinese to learn that chow mein on the menu stands for dishes with a basis of fried noodles, and that the best-known Cantonese chow mein is a mixture of pasta, shrimp (prawns), abalone, mushrooms, bean sprouts, bamboo shoots, lettuce and plenty of flavourings, including garlic. There is also a beef chow mein, or beef stew with noodles.

The typical white marble mortar used to pound the ingredients for a Ligurian pesto *sauce.*

The Indonesian version of pasta is called *bahami*; it is boiled, left to cool, then fried in oil with meat, shrimp and vegetables, and then called *bahami goreng*. Japanese noodles are mainly served with fish- or vegetable-based sauces. A play at the *kabuki* theatre in Tokyo showed a pilgrim coming back from a long journey and telling of his adventures as he noisily eats noodles with chopsticks out of a large bowl — eating noisily is a sign of great enjoyment. In the East pasta is made with flour and eggs or flour and water (sometimes a mixture of wheat and rice flour); and sometimes yam paste is used for noodles to obtain transparent strands like violin strings which cannot ever be overcooked and have almost no flavour at all — at least for anyone used to durum wheat flour pasta. So far I have not been able to taste the *lasagne* made from bread fruit flour mentioned by Marco Polo.

The future

Pasta has featured in the daily life of the Italians for a little over a century, not just as food, but as part of Italian folklore and tradition. Its funnier aspects, such as the difficulty in eating it, and the dramatic contrast between the white of the pasta on the plate and the bright red of a tomato sauce have inspired Italian writers, artists and musicians from Leopardi to Pascoli. There is plenty of evidence of this in the spaghetti museum at Pontedassio, a few miles from Imperia, set up in a house belonging to the Agnesi family. The illustrations in this book show some of the many things it contains: paintings by known and unknown artists (including the wonderful Pulcinella by Michele Cammarano), hundreds of Neapolitan prints and watercolours, popular carvings, caricatures and drawings, kitchen utensils and a whole section dedicated to the development of pasta-making equipment.

Speaking of musicians, it is worth mentioning all the music dedicated to pasta, from the "Tarantella dei Maccheroni" sung by Anna Magnani in the film *La Carozza d'Oro* to the "Spaghetti e buon umore" by the Cetra Quartet, or from the "Valzer delle tagliatelle" by Ravasini to "Spaghetti, pizza e una tazza di caffé" by the popular singer Fred Bongusto. Further research into musical archives would certainly reveal more.

The critical question is still, can pasta maintain its culinary position in the future? There is much cause for optimism; pasta has the advantage of being a very natural product — the best is made with only flour and water; furthermore, it is quick and easy to prepare once you are familiar with a few simple sauces, and you can even use tinned sauce enlivened with a little stock cube. A proof of the virtues of pasta lies in the ease with which it can be prepared after an evening out to make a midnight supper of which everybody approves.

For everyday cooking pasta can be transformed in the simplest ways to make a different dish every night: add herbs, for example, or use *linguine* instead of spaghetti, *lingue di passero* instead of *trenette*. The varieties are so endless you only need to remember the likes and dislikes of family and friends: some people hate big pasta shapes, others won't eat very thin pasta. And yet it is the same food, made with the same ingredients using the same machines and the same drying methods. But it is right to complain that no one packet of pasta tastes like another: they all vary, especially from one shape to the next.

The desire for a slim waistline seems to be the only real enemy of pasta. "A good figure" has never been properly defined by any medical textbooks, but it suggests a graceful body without any flab, spare tires or fat paunch. Dieticians insist that pasta eaten in reasonable quantities can never make you fat, and yet every young woman preoccupied with weight-watching cuts out pasta before anything else.

As in all fields the reputation of pasta is also endangered by low-quality products on the market made with soft wheat flour. It may then be cooked badly and served with a horrid sauce. Some of these dishes have been mentioned earlier, but I must include American cold pasta salads and "summer spaghetti" served straight out of the refrigerator. Genuine Italian pasta should be cooked in boiling water, mixed with very hot sauce and eaten hot — the only variation can be when the dish is baked, such as *lasagne bolognesi* that are browned gently in the oven. This is why Italians look with disfavour on cooked tinned pasta such as spaghetti, *tortellini* and ravioli, although they are popular in other countries, and also on frozen pasta oven-ready in little tinfoil trays. This does not indicate any boycott of commercial pasta: *pasta secca* (dried pasta) has always been acceptable from the factory, even though the great Italian cooking tradition must reject the precooked commercial horrors that are on sale today.

It is necessary to strike a balance — and this is one of the aims of this book — between what is worthwhile from the pasta tradition, including recipes from outside Italy, and what is quick and easy for modern needs. We have included up-to-date versions of old recipes (ingredients such as spices and fats have been modified to suit modern tastes), including some that appear in

Head waiter mixing pasta over a burner.

Opposite page: some of the many types of commercial pasta.

Escoffier's great *Guide Culinaire* written at the beginning of the twentieth century. Although he needs no further introduction or explanation, it is appropriate to recall how this great cook, who was called to the highest rank by one of the fathers of the modern hotel trade, César Ritz, and who organized hotel kitchens along the lines of the scientific division of labour developed in factories, produced such bibles of gastronomy as the *Guide Culinaire*, *Le livre des menus* and *Ma Cuisine*. This is why, although Escoffier's recipes are not always within the Italian tradition, they are well worth trying – the marvellous *timballi à la Grimaldi* or *à la Richepin*, for example. Any chef who manages to make these really does deserve a *cordon bleu* (even though this is only an imaginary decoration, as it derives from the fact that several courtiers to the Sun King – Louis XIV – attempted to win favour with his majesty by trying their hand at cooking. They included the Marquis de Béchamel, the Maréchal de Mirepoix and others, and were all "knights" or Chevaliers de St Louis, and were thus entitled to wear the blue riband of that order.)

As for novelty, it is obviously possible to create something new by reconciling tradition with some of the wiser findings of modern dieticians rather than by combining all sorts of odd ingredients. Uncooked tomato sauce is certainly acceptable (but it must be warmed up in a very hot serving dish so it does not lower the temperature of the pasta), and some sauces based on chopped herbs or vegetables rarely if ever used with pasta before, such as asparagus and artichokes, are an excellent innovation. If any of the more way-out recipes that have been criticized actually appear in this book it is because they are currently very popular, and they answer a modern need.

Perhaps one should occasionally draw the line: why include that hybrid invention quite unconnected with Italian cooking, namely *cannelloni*? But even *cannelloni* are a useful invention, quicker to make and stuff than *tortellini* or *capelletti*, and their high meat and vegetable content compared with the amount of pasta dough used would recommend them to any dietician.

However, I have quite deliberately ignored another recipe often included in the pasta section of certain cookbooks: *crespelle*, or *crêpes* (pancakes), as some Italian restaurants like to call them. The point is that they are made with a batter, not with a real pasta dough. Stuffed pancakes are all very well, but as Kipling said, that is another story.

As for the stuffed pastas mentioned earlier, they will probably come to resemble each other more and more without so many regional distinctions. There are still people in Emilia who swear that their *anolini*, *tortelli*, *raviolacci* or whatever are infinitely superior to the quite identical *guanti* (a Renaissance term) of the neighbouring village. In practice the two main sorts of meat or spinach filling are generally used because they satisfy the modern need for speed and ease in the kitchen. Few people care about some of the older fillings which have now almost disappeared, such as ravioli with a fish filling and *polpacce* or *tortelli* without a pasta case, like a meat-and-vegetable sort of *gnocchi*.

As with all things, the future is in our hands. We must preserve the best of our old traditions and accept new ones if they are useful or attractive, always bearing in mind that cooking and eating make one of the pleasantest ways of bringing together relations and friends. Centuries have shown that pasta itself has all the qualities of a good friend.

I would like to end on the slightly nineteenth-century note that spaghetti still suggests to many Italians, with the greeting of the oft-mentioned and always worthy of mention Duke Ippolito Cavalcanti, Duke of Buonvicino: "Reader, be of good sense and good taste and you will live a happy life."

Massimo Alberini

PASTA & PIZZA

*Above and opposite page: stages in making
a pasta dough and rolling it out by hand, or
with the help of a pasta machine.*

PASTA DOUGH

For 4 servings of egg pasta the normal quantities are $3\frac{1}{4}$ cups (sifted) ($\frac{3}{4}$lb) white flour, 3 whole eggs and a pinch of salt. In some regions a little oil or milk is added to the eggs; in others white flour is combined with or completely replaced by durum wheat flour (semolina). Every sort of flour has different absorbency, so it is sometimes necessary to add more or less flour than the quantity given. Dough to be rolled out by hand should be softer than dough rolled out in a pasta machine; in fact, if a machine is to be used do not knead the dough very much but just feed it through the rollers several times and it will come out smooth and firm.

Put the flour in a mound on a working surface or pastry board, break the eggs in the middle, add a pinch of salt and use a fork to stir in the flour gradually. Then knead with your fingers and the heel of your palm for at least ten minutes until the dough is very elastic (if you cut it you should hear the air bubbles pop). Leave to rest for about fifteen minutes wrapped in a lightly floured cloth. Divide in two (leave the other half still wrapped in the cloth) and roll out the pasta, working from the centre to obtain a fairly thin smooth sheet of dough. Do not let it tear. Leave to dry for a few minutes, but beware of letting it get too dry. Roll up very carefully and cut into whatever type of pasta you want with a very sharp knife. For *tortellini*, *agnolotti*, ravioli, *cannelloni* etc. follow the instructions given in the individual recipe.

STUFFED PASTA

Make the egg pasta dough with flour, eggs, a pinch of salt and a little oil if desired, then roll it out into two fairly thin sheets. Put little mounds of the meat, *ricotta* cheese or vegetable filling at regular intervals on one sheet, brush the space between with beaten egg and water and cover with the second sheet of dough. Press down well with your fingers between each mound of filling, then cut into squares with a serrated edge pasta wheel to obtain ravioli. Alternatively, put the filling at regular intervals apart and cut rounds with a special cutter or the edge of a thin-rimmed glass. Brush with beaten egg and water or just water, and fold over each round to make a little crescent. For *cappellini*, *tortellini* etc. draw the points together and press gently.

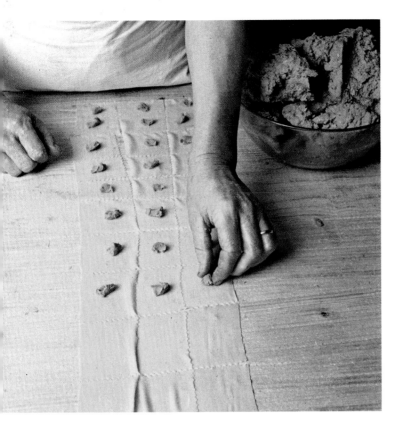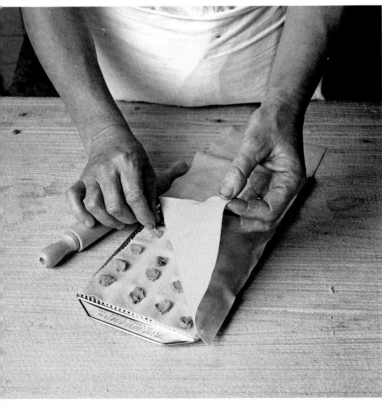

REGIONAL RECIPES

Spaghetti con salsa di pomodoro · SPAGHETTI WITH TOMATO SAUCE

---

5 large firm, ripe tomatoes
4 tablespoons olive oil
¾lb spaghetti
parmesan cheese
salt and pepper
bay leaves

Choose 3 of the firmest tomatoes, plunge them for 1 minute (not longer) in boiling water, and remove the skins. Cut in quarters, remove the seeds and core, then cut each quarter in half lengthwise to obtain 8 sections from each tomato. Use a fork to avoid handling the tomatoes too much as they should be firm, not soft and mushy. Skin the remaining tomatoes, squeeze out the seeds, chop and cook gently for about 20 minutes to obtain a thick sauce. Add 2 tablespoons olive oil just at the end of the cooking period, let it simmer a little longer, then add the remaining oil and the tomato sections. Mix with the spaghetti, which you have cooked in plenty of boiling, salted water, and add a little grated parmesan and freshly ground black pepper to taste. For a stronger flavour leave a few bay leaves to marinate in the oil 24 hours before using.

Serves 4

Trenette al pesto · TRENETTE WITH PESTO SAUCE (Liguria)

about 30 basil leaves
1 tablespoon pine nuts, lightly
   toasted
1 clove garlic
$\frac{1}{4}$ cup grated *pecorino* cheese
$\frac{1}{3}$ cup grated parmesan cheese
4 tablespoons olive oil
1 medium potato
$\frac{3}{4}$lb *trenette* or *linguine*
salt and pepper

Make the *pesto* sauce in advance. Pound the basil in a mortar with the pine nuts and garlic, or purée in a blender. When it is the consistency of mayonnaise transfer to a serving bowl and gently stir in the grated *pecorino* and parmesan, and then the oil, a little at a time. For a more piquant sauce pound a piece of dried red chili pepper with the other ingredients, although this is not part of an authentic *pesto*. Leave to stand for at least 1 hour. Peel and dice the potato and cook in boiling water until nearly done, then add the *trenette*. Drain while the pasta is still firm and chewy, reserving a few tablespoons of the cooking water. Use this to dilute the *pesto*, then pour over the pasta in a hot serving bowl.

Serves 4

Above left : trenette al pesto
Above right : fettuccine al pesto

Lasagne al sugo · LASAGNE WITH MEAT AND TOMATO SAUCE (Liguria)

$2\frac{3}{4}$ cups (sifted) flour
3 eggs
salt
1 onion
1 stick celery
1 small carrot
1 sprig parsley
$\frac{1}{4}$ cup butter
$\frac{3}{4}$lb ground (minced) lean veal or beef
6 tablespoons dry white wine
4 ripe or canned (tinned) peeled
tomatoes
salt and pepper
$\frac{2}{3}$ cup grated parmesan cheese
$\frac{3}{4}$ cup stock

Mix the flour (reserve 1 tablespoon), eggs and a pinch of salt and knead to obtain a smooth elastic dough. Roll out fairly thinly and cut into 2–$2\frac{1}{2}$in squares (which are known as *lasagne* in Genoa). Set aside. Finely chop the onion, celery, carrot and parsley. Melt the butter, add the ground meat and chopped vegetables and cook over a moderate heat, stirring continually for 5 or 6 minutes. Moisten with the wine, raise the heat and let it evaporate uncovered until the smell of the wine is gone. Peel the tomatoes after plunging them in boiling water for 1 minute, squeeze out the seeds and chop coarsely, then add to the meat. Season with salt and freshly ground pepper and allow to simmer, covered, for about 15 minutes. Put the 1 tablespoon flour in a steel or aluminium pan and stir continually over moderate heat until golden brown, then stir in the boiling stock and mix with the meat. Cook covered until the sauce is smooth and thick.

Cook the *lasagne* in plenty of boiling salted water and drain while still firm and chewy. Put layers of pasta in a serving dish, together with the sauce and grated parmesan. Serve very hot.

Serves 4

Below : lasagne al sugo

Piccagge al sugo · PICCAGGE WITH MEAT AND TOMATO SAUCE (Liguria)

2¾ cups (sifted) flour
3 eggs
¾ cup dried mushrooms
¼ cup butter
¾ lb lean veal (whole or cut into small pieces)
1 onion
4 ripe or canned (tinned) peeled tomatoes
salt and pepper
⅔ cup grated parmesan cheese

Mix the flour (reserve 1 tablespoon) with the eggs and a pinch of salt and knead until smooth and elastic. Roll out fairly thinly and leave to dry for a few minutes, then cut into broad strips (known as *piccagge* in the Genoese dialect), laying them out so they do not stick together. Soak the mushrooms in a little warm water for about 20 minutes. Melt the butter in a pan and brown the piece of veal on all sides with the chopped onion, stirring continually. Peel the tomatoes, squeeze out the seeds and chop coarsely (just put canned (tinned) tomatoes through a food mill) and add to the meat, together with the chopped mushrooms. Season with salt and freshly ground pepper and simmer covered for about 15 minutes. Put the 1 tablespoon flour in a pan and stir continually over a moderate heat until brown, then stir into the meat sauce, adding some boiling stock if it seems too dry. Cook covered until the meat is tender. Cook the *piccagge* in plenty of boiling salted water, drain while still firm and mix in a serving dish with the meat sauce and grated parmesan. The veal can be cut in slices and served as a second course with a green salad.

Serves 4

Right: piccagge al sugo

Gasse al sugo · GASSE WITH MEAT AND TOMATO SAUCE (Liguria)

2¾ cups (sifted) flour
3 eggs
¾ cup dried mushrooms
¼ cup butter
¾ lb lean veal
4 ripe or canned (tinned) peeled tomatoes
salt and pepper
⅔ cup grated parmesan cheese

Make the dough as in the previous recipe, but cut into strips ½ in wide and about 4 in long for *gasse*. Press the ends together to make rings or loose knots. Make the sauce and serve up in the same way as for the previous recipe.

Serves 4

Corzetti alla polceverasca · CORZETTI WITH MEAT AND TOMATO SAUCE (Liguria)

2¾ cups (sifted) flour
3 eggs
¾lb lean veal or beef
1 onion
¼ cup butter
4 ripe or canned (tinned) peeled
  tomatoes
salt and pepper
¾ cup stock
⅔ cup grated parmesan cheese

Make a firm pasta dough with the flour, eggs and a pinch of salt and knead until smooth and elastic (make sure you hear the air bubbles pop when you cut it). Roll out fairly thinly and break off pieces about the size of a walnut, then flatten them with your fingertips and pinch in the middle to make little figures of eight – the Genoese *corzetti*. Let them dry a little while making the sauce.

Finely chop the meat and the onion and brown for 5 minutes in the butter. Plunge the tomatoes in boiling water and remove the skins, squeeze out the seeds and chop coarsely (just put canned (tinned) tomatoes through a food mill), then add to the meat. Season with salt and freshly ground pepper and simmer covered for a long time, adding hot stock if necessary. When the meat is completely cooked through the mixture put through a food mill, then re-heat for a minute or two.

Cook the *corzetti* in plenty of boiling salted water. Drain while still quite firm and mix in a hot serving bowl with the parmesan and the sauce.

For the sake of accuracy, it should be mentioned that certain pasta rectangles or circles made with a special cutter are also called *corzetti*.

Serves 4

Maccheroni arrosto · MACARONI AU GRATIN

(Liguria)

2 cloves garlic
1 sprig rosemary
$\frac{1}{4}$ cup butter
$\frac{1}{2}$ lb ground (minced) lean beef or veal
6 tablespoons dry white wine
4 ripe or canned (tinned) peeled
   tomatoes
salt and pepper
$\frac{3}{4}$ cup beef stock
$\frac{2}{3}$ cup grated parmesan cheese
$\frac{3}{4}$ lb macaroni

Finely chop the garlic and rosemary. Melt the butter (reserve 1 tablespoon) and brown the meat, garlic and rosemary for a few minutes, stirring constantly over a moderate heat. Raise the heat and pour in the wine. Let it evaporate, stirring continually, until the smell of the wine is gone. Peel the tomatoes, squeeze out the seeds and chop coarsely (just put canned (tinned) tomatoes through a food mill), then add to the meat with salt and freshly ground pepper. Stir in the hot stock and reducing the heat, simmer covered until the sauce is smooth and thick.

Cook the macaroni in plenty of boiling salted water, drain while still quite firm and arrange in a greased ovenproof dish with layers of sauce and a little grated parmesan. Dot the final layer with butter and bake for about 20 minutes in a moderate oven, until golden brown, then serve very hot in the same dish.

Serves 4

Trofie (gnocchi) al pesto · TROFIE (GNOCCHI) WITH PESTO SAUCE   **(Liguria)**

3¼ cups (sifted) flour
about 30 basil leaves
1 tablespoon pine nuts, toasted
1 clove garlic
¼ cup grated *pecorino* cheese
⅓ cup grated parmesan cheese
4 tablespoons olive oil
salt and pepper

Mix the flour and a pinch of salt with a little water to make a fairly firm dough. Knead until firm and elastic, then break off small pieces about the size of a cherry and press them down on the table to make short fat sticks with pointed ends. Wrap each piece round a thick knitting needle, then remove the needle to obtain a little pasta roll. Cook for a few minutes in plenty of boiling salted water, drain well and mix with the *pesto* sauce, made as in *Trenette al pesto*, page 48.

Serves 4

Above : Trofie (gnocchi) al pesto

Spaghettini col basilico tritato · SPAGHETTINI WITH BASIL   **(Liguria)**

5 large ripe or canned (tinned)
   peeled tomatoes
¼ cup butter
1 tablespoon chopped onion
salt and pepper
¾ lb *spaghettini*
⅔ cup grated parmesan cheese
about 15 finely chopped basil leaves

Break the tomatoes into pieces with your hands and put in a pan (just pour in canned (tinned) tomatoes), then boil for about 30 minutes and put through a food mill. Melt half the butter and when it starts to foam add the chopped onion and cook until soft. Stir in the puréed tomatoes, season with salt and freshly ground pepper and cook over a moderate heat for about 10 minutes. Meanwhile cook the *spaghettini* in plenty of boiling salted water. Drain while still firm and chewy and put in a hot serving dish. Dot with butter and sprinkle with half the parmesan and the chopped basil, then pour over the tomato sauce. Mix well; serve the remaining grated parmesan separately.

Serves 4

Below : spaghettini col basilico tritato

4 large tomatoes
**4 cups mushrooms (preferably
  boletus edulis), sliced**
1 tablespoon oil
½ onion, chopped
parsley
1 clove garlic
salt and pepper
¾ lb *lasagne*
3 tablespoons butter
⅔ cup grated parmesan cheese

Peel the tomatoes and gently squeeze out the seeds and some of the liquid. Clean the mushrooms and slice thinly. Heat the oil and add the chopped onion, parsley and crushed garlic, then the tomatoes cut in strips. (If no tomatoes are available dilute 2 tablespoons tomato paste (purée) with ¾ cup (6 fl oz) boiling stock or water.) Add the mushrooms, season with salt and pepper and cook slowly covered for about ½ hour, or until thick and creamy. Cook the *lasagne* in plenty of boiling salted water, drain and mix in a hot serving dish with slathers of butter, the mushroom sauce and the grated parmesan.

Some people find it more digestible if the oil is stirred into the sauce at the end, and butter is used instead to cook the vegetables.

Serves 4

1 lb spinach
2 anchovy fillets
1 clove garlic
1 sprig parsley
2½ tablespoons pine nuts, finely
   chopped
1 lb *vermicelli*
salt
4 tablespoons olive oil

Cook the spinach in a very little boiling salted water. Wash the anchovies to remove the salt and chop with the clove of garlic, the parsley and cooked spinach. Sauté mixture lightly in the oil, then add the pine nuts and leave to cook for a few minutes. Half-cook the *vermicelli* in plenty of boiling salted water and drain well. Put in a wide ovenproof dish and spread the sauce evenly over the top (it should be fairly liquid to finish cooking the pasta). Bake for about 15 minutes in a hot oven. Parmesan is not served with this dish.

Serves 4

Lasagne al sangue · LASAGNE WITH PIG'S BLOOD (Piedmont)

¼lb sweetbreads
1 sprig parsley
½ onion
2 tablespoons olive oil
2 tablespoons butter
½lb fresh pork sausage meat
¾lb fresh *lasagne*
salt
1¼ cups pig's blood
6 tablespoons milk
⅔ cup grated parmesan cheese

Blanch the sweetbreads in lightly salted boiling water. Chop the parsley and onion and brown in the oil and butter with the sausage meat and chopped sweetbreads. Cook over a low heat covered for about 30 minutes. Meanwhile cook the *lasagne* in boiling salted water and drain when half-cooked. Put the pig's blood and milk in a broad pan and when they are hot add the *lasagne* and stir very gently over a moderate heat until the blood is thick and dark (but it should not coagulate). Pour in the sweetbread mixture, remove from the heat and sprinkle with grated parmesan. Mix well and serve very hot.

Serves 4

Above : lasagne al sangue

Tajarin all'albese coi fegatini · TAGLIATELLE WITH CHICKEN LIVERS (Piedmont)

2¾ cups (sifted) flour
3 eggs
¼ cup butter
¼lb chicken livers
1 tablespoon meat extract (or 1
    bouillon (stock) cube)
nutmeg
⅔ cup grated parmesan cheese
salt and pepper
1 white truffle

Make the dough with the flour and eggs, kneading well until it is smooth and elastic, then roll out very thinly and cut into *tajarin* or *tagliatelle* about ¼in wide. Put the butter in a small pan and when it starts to foam, brown the finely sliced chicken livers for 2 or 3 minutes. Stir in the bouillon (stock) cube or meat extract dissolved in 4 tablespoons hot water, season with salt and a pinch of nutmeg to taste. Boil uncovered over a moderate heat to reduce a little. Cook the *tagliatelle* in plenty of boiling salted water, drain while still firm and chewy and put in a hot serving dish. Mix with the sauce, sprinkle with grated parmesan and freshly ground pepper, then top with thin slices of truffle.

Serves 4

Below left : tajarin all'albese coi fegatini

Tagliatelline con la fonduta · TAGLIATELLINE WITH FONDUE (Piedmont)

1½ cups *fontina* cheese, thinly sliced
½ cup milk
2 tablespoons butter
3 egg yolks
salt and pepper
¾lb *tagliatelline*
1 white truffle

Put the sliced *fontina* in a pan, pour over the lukewarm milk and leave to stand for at least 2 hours. Melt the butter in a stainless steel pan, then add the drained *fontina* with 2 tablespoons of the milk, beating gently with a whisk over low heat until the cheese has completely melted. Raise the heat and beat in the egg yolks one at a time to make a smooth, creamy sauce. Season with salt and pepper.

Cook the *tagliatelline* in plenty of boiling salted water, drain well and put in a hot serving dish. Pour over the fondue sauce and mix well. Top with thinly sliced truffle.

Serves 4

Below right : tagliatelline con la fonduta

Gnocchi alla piemontese · GNOCCHI WITH BUTTER AND SAGE   (Piedmont)

5 or 6 medium potatoes
1¾ cups (sifted) flour
salt
¼ cup butter
a few sage leaves
⅔ cup grated parmesan cheese

Peel the potatoes and steam in a small amount of salted water. When they are cooked, drain and leave uncovered on the fire for 15 seconds. Then rapidly put through a food mill or potato ricer so they fall in a mound on a pastry board or working surface. Gradually work in the flour and 1 teaspoon salt, then knead well to obtain a smooth elastic dough. (You may need to use more or less flour depending on the quality of the potatoes.) Roll out and cut off squares, then roll these into little 1 in pieces and press against the back of a curved grater or fork to obtain the traditional *gnocchi* shape (see photograph). They cook better if they are concave. Cook in plenty of boiling salted water for a few minutes over a good heat, then remove with a slotted spoon and put in individual dishes with several tablespoons of butter melted with some sage leaves. Sprinkle with grated parmesan.

Serves 4

Above : gnocchi alla piemontese

Tagliatelli al sugo · TAGLIATELLI WITH HAM AND TOMATO SAUCE   (Piedmont)

1⅓ cups grated parmesan cheese
3¼ cups (sifted) flour
2 eggs
2 egg yolks
1 slice cooked ham
1 stick celery
1 small carrot
¼ cup butter
2¼ cups canned (tinned) peeled
  tomatoes
salt and pepper

Mix ⅓ cup (1oz) of the parmesan with the flour and knead in the eggs and egg yolks to obtain a firm, elastic dough, then roll out very thin. Leave to dry a little and cut into wide strips about 1½in wide. Make these into *tagliatelli* by piling up a few at a time and cutting into strips not more than ¼in wide. Dice the ham and finely chop the celery and carrot. Heat half the butter and cook the ham and chopped vegetables until soft, then add the sieved tomatoes. Season with salt and pepper and cook over a low heat until thick. Cook the *tagliatelli* in plenty of boiling salted water, drain and place in a very hot serving dish. Dot with the remaining butter and pour over the sauce. Serve the grated parmesan separately.

Serves 4

Below : tagliatelli al sugo

Pizzoccheri della valtellina · PIZZOCCHERI WITH CABBAGE AND POTATOES (Lombardy)

1¾ cups corn meal (maize flour)
scant 1 cup white flour
1 egg
¾ cup milk
3 medium potatoes
3 large cabbage leaves
⅔ cup firm white *valtellina* or Bel
   Paese cheese, finely sliced
¼ cup butter
3 or 4 sage leaves
salt and pepper

Mix the corn meal (maize flour) and white flour and make into a fairly firm dough with the egg, milk and a little water if necessary. Roll out not too thin and cut into long strips about 2in wide. Set aside. Peel and dice the potatoes; cut the cabbage into thin strips and cook together in boiling salted water. When the cabbage is almost tender add the *pizzoccheri* and cook over a good heat. Drain when the pasta is still firm and chewy and put layers of *pizzoccheri* and vegetables in a deep serving dish, covering each layer with thin slices of cheese. Melt the butter with the sage and pour over the pasta, adding freshly ground pepper to taste.

Serves 4

Gnocchi di zucca mantovani · PUMPKIN GNOCCHI (Lombardy)

2 cups pumpkin purée, fresh or
    canned (tinned)
$1\frac{1}{4}$ cups (sifted) flour
salt
5 tablespoons butter
$\frac{2}{3}$ cup grated parmesan cheese

Peel the pumpkin and remove the green part under the skin, then cut the rest into large pieces and boil in lightly salted water. When tender put through a food mill, then put the purée on a pastry board or working surface with some of the flour and a pinch of salt. Knead well to obtain a fairly soft and elastic dough, gradually adding more flour; the quantity needed will rather depend on the ripeness and consistency of the pumpkin. Divide into little pieces 1in long, then press them against the curved back of a fork or grater to obtain the traditional *gnocchi* shape, and cook in plenty of boiling salted water a few at a time, to prevent them sticking together. Remove with a slotted spoon as they rise to the surface, put in individual dishes, pour over melted butter and sprinkle with parmesan. Serve very hot.

Serves 4

Bigoli co' le sardele · BIGOLI (WHOLE WHEAT SPAGHETTI) WITH SARDINES (Veneto)

2¾ cups (sifted) whole wheat flour
2 eggs
4 salt-cured or canned (tinned) sardines
3 tablespoons oil

Make a dough with the whole wheat flour and eggs, adding water as necessary, then knead well and put through a special "bigoli" hand press. If the equipment is unavailable, cook ¾lb commercial whole wheat spaghetti in the usual way. Wash the sardines to remove the salt, fillet them if necessary, then chop in small pieces. Heat the sardines in the oil, then crush with a fork in the pan to make a smooth sauce. Mix with the hot *bigoli*.

Grated parmesan is not served with this dish.

Serves 4

Above left: bigoli co' le sardele

Bigoli in salsa · BIGOLI WITH ANCHOVIES (Veneto)

4 salt-cured or canned (tinned) anchovies
1 medium onion
3 tablespoons oil
1 sprig parsley
salt and pepper
¾lb *bigoli* (whole wheat spaghetti)

Rinse the salt from the anchovies and fillet if necessary, then chop with the onion. Put in a pan with the oil and cook very gently, covered, until soft. Add the chopped parsley and some freshly ground pepper, then continue cooking until the sauce is thick and smooth. Make the *bigoli* as in the previous recipe or use commercial whole wheat spaghetti. Cook in plenty of boiling salted water, drain and serve with the hot anchovy sauce.

No grated parmesan is served with this dish.

Serves 4

Above right: bigoli in salsa

Papparelle e fegatini · PAPPARELLE WITH CHICKEN LIVERS (Veneto)

¼lb chicken livers
2¼ cups (sifted) flour
3 eggs
1 tablespoon butter
salt and pepper
4½ cups chicken, beef or, better still, capon stock
⅔ cup grated parmesan cheese

Clean the chicken livers well and remove any green parts, then wash and chop in small pieces. Mix the flour, eggs and a pinch of salt, then knead until smooth and elastic. Roll out fairly thinly, leave to dry a little, then roll up and cut in strips about ¼in wide, known as *papparelle*. Melt the butter in a small pan and when it starts to foam add the chicken livers, season with salt and pepper and brown on all sides. Pour into the boiling stock together with the *papparelle* and cook until the pasta has absorbed nearly all the stock. Serve grated parmesan separately.

If you use commercial pasta rather than homemade, begin with three cups of stock and add the remainder only if necessary, otherwise you may end up with a plate of soup, rather than a dish of pasta.

Serves 4

Below: papparelle e fegatini

Bigoli co' l'anara · BIGOLI WITH DUCK   (Veneto)

1 duckling
1 onion
1 stick celery
1 small carrot
¼ cup butter
a few sage leaves
salt and pepper
¾ lb *bigoli* (whole wheat spaghetti)
⅔ cup grated parmesan cheese
stock from duck

Clean and wash the duck, being especially careful to remove as much fat as possible, reserving the liver and giblets. Boil duck gently in lightly salted water with the onion, celery and carrot until duck is tender (1–1½ hours). Skim fat from stock. Melt the butter with the sage, then brown the very finely chopped duck liver and giblets. Moisten with a little duck stock, season with salt and pepper and simmer for about 15 minutes over a low heat. Make the *bigoli* as in *Bigoli co' le sardele*, page 64, or use commercial whole wheat spaghetti. Cook the *bigoli* in the duck stock, drain and put in a deep serving dish, then mix well with the liver and giblet sauce, sprinkle with parmesan and serve very hot. Serve the duck as a second course with any suitable sauce. For a lighter dish remove the duck skin before cooking, as this is the fatty part.

Serves 4

Right: bigoli co' l'anara

Gnocchi alla "pastissada" · GNOCCHI WITH MEAT AND TOMATO SAUCE   (Veneto)

5 or 6 medium potatoes
1¾ cups (sifted) flour
¾–1 lb well-aged horse meat or
    stewing beef
¼ cup butter
1 tablespoon olive oil
5 large ripe or canned (tinned)
    peeled tomatoes
¾ cup old red wine
2 onions, chopped
grated parmesan cheese
salt and pepper
pinch cinnamon

Cook the potatoes, remove the skins then put through a potato ricer or food mill so they fall on a pastry board or working surface in a mound. Gradually mix in the flour to obtain a smooth soft dough, using as little flour as possible; new potatoes absorb more than old ones. Pinch into pieces about 1 in long, then press them against the back of a curved grater or fork to obtain the traditional *gnocchi* shape. Arrange on a cloth so they do not stick together and then make the meat sauce or *pastissada*. Cut the meat into small pieces and brown well in the butter and oil for a few minutes over a high heat. Peel the tomatoes and squeeze out the seeds. Stir the wine into the meat, then add the tomatoes and chopped onion. Cover and leave to cook for 3 or 4 hours until the meat is fork tender.

Cook the *gnocchi* in plenty of boiling salted water and remove with a slotted spoon as they come to the surface. Serve them in individual dishes covered with the meat sauce, grated parmesan and freshly ground pepper and cinnamon to taste.

Serves 4

Gnocchi alla veneta · GNOCCHI WITH TOMATO SAUCE   (Veneto)

5 or 6 medium potatoes
1¼ cups (sifted) flour
2 eggs
5 large ripe or canned (tinned)
    peeled tomatoes
¼ cup butter
salt
grated parmesan cheese

Cook the potatoes, peel and put through a potato ricer or food mill so they fall in a mixing bowl with the flour. Beat in the 2 eggs and a pinch of salt, then put the dough on a pastry board or working surface and knead to obtain a smooth, soft, elastic dough. Make into small rolls then cut into pieces about ¾ in long and press them against the curve of a fork or cheese grater to give them the traditional *gnocchi* shape. Leave well separated so they do not stick together. Put the tomatoes through a food mill, then place in a pan with the butter and salt to taste. Simmer uncovered over a moderate heat to obtain a smooth sauce. Cook the *gnocchi* in plenty of boiling salted water and remove with a slotted spoon as they rise to the surface. Put on individual plates and cover each serving with about 2 tablespoons tomato sauce and a little grated parmesan. Serve immediately.

Serves 4

Above left : gnocchi alla veneta

Gnocchi alla veronese · GNOCCHI WITH CHEESE AND SUGAR   (Veneto)

5 or 6 medium potatoes
1¾ cups (sifted) flour
salt
⅓ cup butter
sugar
1 teaspoon cinnamon
⅔ cup grated parmesan cheese

Make the *gnocchi* as in *gnocchi alla veneta* above, except no eggs are used in this recipe so the quantity of flour is increased to make a firm dough. Cook in plenty of boiling salted water for about 3 minutes, then remove with a slotted spoon as they come to the surface. Let drain then put on heated individual plates. Heat the butter in a small pan and when it starts to brown pour about 2 tablespoons on to each serving, sprinkle with a little sugar and cinnamon and plenty of grated parmesan.

Serves 4

Above right : gnocchi alla veronese

Bigoli coi rovinazzi · BIGOLI WITH CHICKEN GIBLETS   (Veneto)

¼ lb chicken livers
¼ lb chicken giblets
¾ lb *bigoli* (whole wheat spaghetti)
salt
¼ cup butter
sage leaves
chicken stock
⅔ cup grated parmesan cheese

Clean and finely chop the chicken livers and giblets. Cook the *bigoli* in plenty of boiling salted water (see *bigoli* recipe on p. 64). Heat the butter with a few sage leaves and when it browns add the giblets (in the Veneto the *rovinazzi* include all the extraneous parts of the chicken, such as the feet or wings), and leave to cook for about 30 minutes, adding a little stock if necessary. Add the chicken livers right at the end so they are soft and tender. Drain the *bigoli* while still firm and chewy, then mix with the sauce and sprinkle with grated parmesan. Serve very hot.

Serves 4

Below : bigoli coi rovinazzi

Canederli · DUMPLINGS (Trentino-Alto Adige)

4 eggs
¾ cup milk
6 cups stale bread, diced (cubed)
½ cup unsmoked bacon or raw ham, finely chopped
2 slices salami, finely chopped
1 medium onion
1 sprig parsley
3 tablespoons flour
salt and pepper
¼ cup butter
grated parmesan cheese

Beat the eggs with the milk and a little salt. Dice the bread and soak for about 20 minutes in the milk mixture, stirring frequently and gently with a wooden spoon so all the milk is absorbed. Heat the diced bacon or ham and salami in a small pan over a low heat, together with the chopped onion and parsley, drain most of the fat then pour into the bread and milk mixture. Stir gently, slowly adding the flour, season with salt and freshly ground black pepper to taste.

Take a large spoonful of the mixture and roll it in your wet hands, or else shape it with two spoons to obtain an egg-shaped ball. Drop this first dumpling into gently boiling salted water to see if it holds together; if not add a few more spoonfuls of flour to the rest of the mixture before making the remaining balls. Lower them into the boiling water with a large slotted spoon and remove as they come to the surface, then put on individual plates and serve with melted butter and grated cheese. Alternatively, these *canederli* can be served in a clear soup, but it needs to be very highly flavoured and worthy of these delicious dumplings.

Serves 4

Above: canederli in consommé and on their own.

70

Tagliatelle "smalzade" · TAGLIATELLE WITH WINE AND CREAM   (Trentino-Alto Adige)

2¾ cups (sifted) flour
3 eggs
1lb lean veal cut in pieces
¼ cup butter
1 medium onion
6 tablespoons white wine
stock *or*
1 teaspoon meat extract
salt and pepper
6 tablespoons cream
⅔ cup grated parmesan cheese

Make a pasta dough with the flour (reserve 1 tablespoon), eggs and a pinch of salt, then knead well until it pops when you cut it. If the dough seems too dry add a few tablespoons warm water. Roll out evenly but not too thinly, leave to dry for a little while, then cut into *tagliatelle* about ¼in wide. Roll the piece of veal in the remaining flour. Melt the butter in a large skillet and brown the veal on all sides along with the onion cut in quarters. Moisten with the wine, let it cook rapidly until you cannot smell the wine any more, then add a little stock. When the veal is almost cooked reduce heat, season with salt and freshly ground pepper and stir in the cream.

Cook the *tagliatelle* in plenty of boiling salted water, drain, then mix with the veal sauce and some grated parmesan. Serve the cut-up meat, either as a second course with some salad or with the *tagliatelle*. For a lighter dish – it is delicious even without the cream.

Serves 4

Garganelli · **GARGANELLI WITH MEAT AND TOMATO SAUCE**   (Emilia-Romagna)

2¾ **cups (sifted) flour**
3 **eggs**
⅔ **cup grated parmesan cheese**
1 **small carrot**
1 **medium onion**
1 **stick celery**
½ **cup Canadian (unsmoked) bacon,
   chopped**
3 **tablespoons butter**
½**lb ground (minced) veal or beef**
6 **tablespoons dry white wine**
1½ **cups canned (tinned) peeled
   tomatoes**
2 **chicken livers**
salt and pepper

Mix the flour, eggs and half the parmesan and knead to obtain a smooth, elastic dough. Roll out fairly thinly, then cut into 2½in squares. Hold one corner round a greased stick the diameter of your little finger and wrap the square around it diagonally (the stick should be less than 1 in thick), then roll off on to the "comb", a special ribbed metal instrument (or use an ordinary comb) to obtain ribbed tubes with slanting ends like *penne*. Chop the carrot, onion, celery and bacon. Heat 1 tablespoon (½oz) butter and when it starts to brown add the chopped vegetables and ground (minced) meat. Brown for 4 or 5 minutes, then pour over the wine and let it cook over a good heat until you cannot smell it any more. Put the tomatoes through a food mill, then add to the meat. Season with salt and pepper and cook gently uncovered until smooth and thick. Just before removing the pan from the heat add the well cleaned chopped chicken livers.

Cook the *garganelli* in plenty of boiling salted water, drain and mix with hunks of butter, the meat sauce and the remaining parmesan.

Serves 4

Lasagne alla ferrarese · LASAGNE WITH MEAT AND TOMATO SAUCE   (Emilia-Romagna)

1 small onion
½ carrot
1 stick celery
**1 cup raw prosciutto with its fat,
  chopped**
¼ cup butter
½lb ground (minced) lean beef
6 tablespoons dry white wine
**2¼ cups canned (tinned) peeled
  tomatoes**
salt and pepper
¾lb *lasagne*
**2¼ cups *béchamel sauce (see lasagne
  verdi*, page 76)**
1⅓ cups grated parmesan cheese

Finely chop the onion, carrot, celery and prosciutto. Heat the butter in a casserole or terracotta dish and add the chopped vegetables and prosciutto and cook together for several minutes on a low flame, then add the beef and brown on all sides. Raise the heat, add the wine and let it evaporate quickly. Put the tomatoes through a food mill then add to the meat. Lower the heat, season with salt and freshly ground pepper, cover the pan and cook over a low heat for about 1 hour adding some stock or water if it seems too dry.

    Cook the *lasagne* in plenty of boiling salted water and remove from the heat while still firm, then rinse under the cold tap. Grease an ovenproof dish and put in alternate layers of *lasagne*, meat sauce and a few tablespoons of *béchamel* sauce with a sprinkling of grated parmesan. Dot the final layer of *béchamel* with butter and bake at about 400° for 30 minutes. Serve very hot.

Serves 4

Tagliatelle alla romagnola · TAGLIATELLE WITH TOMATO SAUCE (Emilia-Romagna)

1 sprig parsley
1 clove garlic
4 large tomatoes
4 tablespoons olive oil
salt and pepper
¾lb *tagliatelle*

Chop the parsley and garlic; squeeze the seeds from the tomatoes and cut in pieces. Put the oil in a pan and cook the vegetables with some salt and freshly ground pepper over a medium heat to make a thick sauce. Put through a food mill. Cook the *tagliatelle* in plenty of boiling salted water, drain while still firm and put in a deep serving dish. Pour over the tomato sauce and serve immediately.

Grated cheese is not usually served with this dish. You can also add a little olive oil to the *tagliatelle* after draining them to make them more slippery and light; however, some people do not like the flavour of uncooked oil.

Serves 4

Above left: tagliatelle alla romagnola

Tagliatelle col prosciutto · TAGLIATELLE WITH RAW PROSCIUTTO (Emilia-Romagna)

2¾ cups (sifted) flour
3 eggs
¼lb raw prosciutto, cut in strips
3 tablespoons butter
salt and pepper
⅔ cup grated parmesan cheese

Make a pasta dough with the flour and eggs and roll out thinly, then cut into *tagliatelle* about ¼in wide. Cook for a few minutes in plenty of boiling salted water. Cook the prosciutto gently in the butter, but do not let it brown. Drain the *tagliatelle* while still firm and chewy and add to the butter and ham; stir for a few minutes over a low heat so the pasta absorbs all the flavour, season with salt and freshly ground pepper, then remove from the heat and stir in the grated parmesan. Serve immediately.

Serves 4

Above right: tagliatelle col prosciutto

Gramigna con la salsiccia · GRAMIGNA WITH ITALIAN SAUSAGE (Emilia-Romagna)

6 large ripe or canned (tinned)
    peeled tomatoes
½lb Italian or any fresh pork sausages
¾lb *gramigna* or *bucatini*
1 cup grated parmesan cheese

Plunge the tomatoes in boiling water and remove the skins, squeeze out the seeds and some of the liquid, then chop coarsely. Wash the sausages, prick with a fork in several places, then put in a pan with the tomatoes and bring to a boil. Lower the heat and simmer covered for about 30 minutes. Remove from the heat and gently skin the sausages, then cut in several pieces and return to the pan to keep hot. Cook the pasta in plenty of boiling salted water, drain while still firm and mix with the hot sauce. Serve grated parmesan separately.

Serves 4

Below: gramigna con la salsiccia

Strichetti · STRICHETTI (Emilia-Romagna)

3 eggs
2¾ cups (sifted) flour
1⅓ cups grated parmesan cheese
4½ cups strong beef stock
salt
pinch nutmeg

Mix the eggs, flour and ½ cup (1½oz) grated parmesan together and knead into a smooth elastic dough. Roll out not too thinly and cut with a pasta wheel into little 1in diamonds. Take each diamond by the longest points and join these points by pressing them together. Then join the shorter points in the same manner underneath. Cook for a few minutes in the boiling stock and serve with the remaining grated parmesan and a pinch of grated nutmeg.

Serves 4

Above : strichetti

Lasagne verdi · GREEN LASAGNE WITH MEAT SAUCE (Emilia-Romagna)

½lb spinach
scant 3 cups (sifted) flour
2 eggs
½ cup butter
2 cups milk
salt and white pepper
grated nutmeg
½ carrot
1 small onion
1 stalk celery
½ cup ground (minced) beef or veal
beef stock (optional)
½ cup chopped raw prosciutto, lean and fat
1⅓ cups grated parmesan cheese

Wash and cook the spinach with very little water. Drain well, squeezing out any excess liquid, put through a food mill and set aside. Put the flour on a pastry board or working surface and mix with the spinach purée and the eggs. Knead well until smooth and elastic, then roll out fairly thinly and cut into strips the length of the dish in which you will bake the *lasagne*. Set aside. Make *béchamel* sauce as follows: Heat 2 tablespoons (1oz) butter and when it starts to foam stir in 2 tablespoons (1 oz) flour and stir continually until the flour is a lovely gold colour. Gradually pour in the hot, but not boiling milk while stirring constantly, season with salt and freshly ground pepper and continue to stir constantly, especially when it is almost boiling, over a low heat for about 15–20 minutes. Add a little grated nutmeg to taste. Remove from the heat when the *béchamel* sauce is smooth and thick. If the sauce is too runny return to the heat with a small piece of butter kneaded with some flour and stir well until smooth.

Chop the carrot, onion and celery into a fine dice. Heat ¼ cup (2oz) butter and cook the chopped vegetables for a few minutes, then add the ground (minced) beef. Season with salt and freshly ground pepper and cook slowly, adding a little water, or better still some stock, if the mixture seems too dry. When it is quite thick add the chopped prosciutto.

Cook the *lasagne* in plenty of boiling salted water, drain while still firm and lay flat on a clean cloth. Liberally grease an ovenproof dish and line with a strip of pasta, then put in alternate layers of meat sauce, *béchamel* (if the sauce has got lumpy while cooling just stir briefly over low heat), and some grated parmesan. End with a layer of pasta, then *béchamel*. Sprinkle with grated parmesan and 2 tablespoons (1oz) melted butter. Bake in a hot oven for about 30 minutes and serve very hot in the same dish.

Serves 4

Below : lasagne verdi

Pasticcio di maccheroni all'uso di Romagna
MACARONI AU GRATIN WITH MUSHROOMS AND SWEETBREADS

2 cups *béchamel* sauce
¾ cup dried mushrooms
¼ lb sweetbreads
¼ lb raw prosciutto, cut in strips
¾ lb macaroni
¼ cup butter
salt and pepper
1 small black truffle (optional)
nutmeg
1⅓ cups grated parmesan cheese

Make the *béchamel* sauce as in the recipe for *lasagne verdi*, page 76. Soak the mushrooms in warm water for about 30 minutes. Blanch the sweetbreads in boiling water, remove the outer membrane and chop coarsely. Cut the prosciutto into narrow strips. Cook the macaroni in plenty of boiling salted water, drain well and spread out on a cloth. Melt the butter and when it starts to brown add the sweetbreads. Season with salt and a little freshly ground pepper and stir in half the *béchamel*, then the mushrooms and prosciutto and some very finely sliced truffle. Add a little grated nutmeg to taste. Butter an ovenproof dish and put in layers of macaroni covered with a few tablespoons of the sauce, some slathers of butter and some of the remaining *béchamel*. Sprinkle the final layer with grated parmesan, dot with butter and bake in a moderate oven for about 20 minutes. Serve hot in the same dish.

Serves 4

Above: pasticcio di maccheroni all'uso di Romagna

Maccheroni alla bolognese · MACARONI WITH BOLOGNESE MEAT SAUCE

1 small onion
1 small stalk celery
1 small carrot
1 cup Canadian (unsmoked) bacon
   or Italian *pancetta*, chopped
¼ cup butter
¼ lb ground (minced) lean veal
1 teaspoon flour
1 cup stock
salt and pepper
pinch nutmeg or cloves
6 tablespoons cream
1 chicken liver
¾ lb *maccheroni rigati* or *penne rigate*
⅔ cup grated parmesan cheese

Chop the onion, celery, carrot and bacon. Melt the butter and gently brown the chopped vegetables with the veal, stirring gently over low heat so the meat does not stick to the pan. Stir in 1 scant teaspoon flour, then the stock (or a bouillon cube with a cup of warm water). Season carefully, with only a little salt as the bacon may be salty, and with some freshly ground black pepper, a pinch of grated nutmeg or ground cloves to taste. Cook over a fairly low heat, stirring occasionally for about 30 minutes. Just before you remove the pan from the heat stir in the cream and the chopped chicken liver. Cook the macaroni in plenty of boiling salted water, drain while quite firm and put in a serving dish with the meat sauce (which should be fairly liquid). Mix well and serve very hot. Serve grated parmesan separately.

Serves 4

Below: maccheroni alla bolognese

Pappardelle sulla lepre · PAPPARDELLE WITH HARE (Tuscany)

$3\frac{1}{4}$ cups (sifted) flour
3 eggs
1 egg yolk
$\frac{1}{4}$ cup unsmoked bacon or Italian
   pancetta, chopped
$\frac{1}{2}$ onion
1 stick celery
1 small carrot
2 sprigs parsley
3 tablespoons butter
4 hare legs
2 hare kidneys
1 tablespoon tomato paste (purée)
stock
salt and pepper
grated parmesan cheese

Make a pasta dough with the flour (reserve 1 tablespoon), eggs and egg yolk and knead until smooth and elastic. Roll out and cut into strips about 1 in wide. Set aside to dry a little, then cut into *pappardelle* about 1 in wide. Chop the bacon, onion, celery, carrot and parsley. Heat the butter in a pan and brown the chopped vegetables. Dredge the hare and kidneys in the remaining flour and brown on all sides. Add the tomato paste (purée) diluted with a little stock. Chop the kidney, season with salt and pepper and cook until the meat is tender, adding a little stock as the liquid dries out. Remove the hare and keep warm. Cook the *pappardelle* in plenty of boiling salted water, drain well and mix with the sauce in a deep, well heated serving bowl. Put a joint of hare on each helping and serve grated parmesan separately, as it is not always appreciated with this dish.

Serves 4

Pappardelle all'aretina · PAPPARDELLE WITH DUCK (Tuscany)

$\frac{3}{4}$ lb *pappardelle*
1 duckling
$\frac{1}{4}$ cup raw prosciutto, finely chopped
1 medium onion
1 stick celery
1 small carrot
2 tablespoons butter
salt and pepper
1 tablespoon concentrated tomato
   paste (purée) 1 tablespoon

Make the *pappardelle* as in the previous recipe (*pappardelle sulla lepre*), but cut the strips of pasta with an indented pasta wheel to give them a frilly edge.

Clean and wash the duckling well removing as much fat as possible. Chop the prosciutto, onion, celery and carrot into a fine dice. Put the butter in a pan with the duck and its liver. Brown on all sides, then add the chopped vegetables. Season with salt and pepper to taste, then cook the duck over a moderate heat, covered, adding the stock mixed with the tomato paste (purée). When almost cooked remove the liver, crush with a fork and stir into the sauce in the pan.

Cook the *pappardelle* in plenty of boiling, salted water, drain while still firm and mix with the duck sauce. Serve the duck itself as a second course, accompanied with a green salad.

Serves 4

Right: pappardelle all'aretina

Lasagne al basilico · LASAGNE WITH BASIL (Tuscany)

1 cup grated *sardo* or parmesan
   cheese
about 20 basil leaves
10 walnut kernels
2 tablespoons olive oil
¾lb *lasagne*
salt

Pound the cheese in a mortar with the basil and walnuts and gradually mix in the oil while still pounding, or do it all in an electric blender. Cook the *lasagne* in plenty of boiling salted water, drain while still firm and mix with the basil. This easily prepared dish has a lovely piquant flavour.

Serves 4

Spaghetti con sugo di seppie · SPAGHETTI WITH CUTTLEFISH SAUCE (Tuscany)

2 cuttlefish or squid, about 10–14oz
1 sprig parsley
1 clove garlic
1½ cups breadcrumbs
4 tablespoons olive oil
salt and pepper
1 medium onion
3 tablespoons concentrated tomato
   paste (purée)
¾lb spaghetti

Remove the outer skin and central bone from the cuttlefish or squid, and also the ink bag, intestines, eyes and mouth. Chop the parsley, garlic and the tentacles, add breadcrumbs and moisten with 1 tablespoon oil; season with salt and pepper and use this mixture to stuff the cuttlefish or squid, then sew up. Chop the onion and put in a pan with the remaining oil. When it starts to brown add the squid, season with a little salt and brown on all sides, then leave to cook for at least 3 hours, gradually adding the tomato paste (purée) diluted with some warm water. Cook the spaghetti in plenty of boiling salted water, drain and mix with the squid sauce. Serve the squid or cuttlefish as a second course with a mixed salad.

Serves 4

Above: spaghetti con sugo di seppie

Pasta alla cacciatora · PASTA HUNTER'S STYLE (Tuscany)

2 teal or other wild duck
1 small carrot, sliced
1 stick celery, chopped
1 sprig parsley
salt
¾lb short pasta, e.g. *penne*, *lumache*,
   nocciole, *paternostri*
¼ cup butter
⅔ cup grated parmesan cheese

Teal live in marshy fenlands and are similar to duck, only smaller. They usually weigh 8–10 oz, like pigeon, but they have a duck's webbed feet and flat bill.
   Draw and clean the teal, burn off any remaining pin feathers, remove and discard the feet and head, and wash well. Put the teal in a pan with water, the livers, carrot, celery, parsley and a little salt. Cook until tender, then bone and chop the meat with the livers. Cook the pasta in the teal stock. Drain well, mix with melted butter, the chopped teal and plenty of grated parmesan. Serve very hot. This is a very delicate and attractive dish.

Serves 4

Below: pasta alla cacciatora

Testaroli al pesto · TESTAROLI WITH PESTO SAUCE (Tuscany)

2¾ cups (sifted) flour
salt
lard
1 sprig basil
1 clove garlic
½ cup grated *pecorino* cheese
4 tablespoons oil
grated parmesan cheese

Mix enough water with the flour and a little salt to make a fairly runny batter. This batter was originally poured into earthenware *testi* or flat pans – hence the name *testaroli* – but nowadays cast-iron pans about 10–12in in diameter are used instead. The *testi* had a lid; they were covered in hot coals so the pasta cooked in 4 or 5 minutes. Now the *testaroli* are made like ordinary pancakes in an ordinary cast-iron pan: use a little lard to grease the bottom of the pan and fry the batter on both sides. Set aside. These can be prepared in advance.

For the sauce pound basil, garlic, and *pecorino* cheese in a mortar and gradually add the olive oil, or else purée all the ingredients in a blender. Boil some water in a large pan and gently slip in the *testaroli*. Remove from the heat and leave the pan to stand for 4 or 5 minutes to heat rather than cook the pancakes. Remove them gently from the pan with a flat spatula. Cut in thin strips and put in a hot serving dish, then pour over the *pesto* sauce and a little grated parmesan.

Serves 4

Left: testaroli being cooked in a testo

Spaghetti con il tartufo nero · SPAGHETTI WITH BLACK TRUFFLE (Umbria)

1 black truffle, about the size of an egg
2 anchovy fillets
4 tablespoons olive oil
1 sprig parsley
¾lb spaghetti
salt

Clean the truffle very well: it should be brushed hard, but never washed. Cut in very thin slices. Wash and chop the anchovies. Mash them in a bowl with a fork, gradually adding the oil a little at a time, then add the truffle and the chopped parsley. Cook the spaghetti in plenty of boiling salted water, drain while still firm and chewy and mix in a serving dish with this wonderfully tasty sauce, which requires *no* extras like grated parmesan.

Serves 4

Tagliolini alla francescana · TAGLIOLINI WITH TOMATO SAUCE (Umbria)

1 medium onion
1 small carrot
1 stalk celery
¼ cup butter
1 sprig parsley
1 sprig thyme
5 large ripe or canned (tinned) peeled tomatoes
salt and pepper
¾lb *tagliolini*
⅔ cup grated parmesan cheese

Chop the onion, carrot and celery into a fine dice. Melt the butter in a big pan and cook the chopped vegetables over low heat for about 6 minutes. Put tomatoes through a food mill and add to the pan with the chopped parsley and thyme. Raise the heat and cook for about 15 minutes covered, until the sauce thickens. Season with salt and pepper. Cook the *tagliolini* in plenty of salted water, then drain, leaving a little water on them. Mix very well with the sauce in a deep hot serving bowl. Sprinkle over half the grated parmesan and stir again. Serve the remaining parmesan separately.

Serves 4

2¾ cups (sifted) flour
1 scant cup finely ground durum
   wheat flour
3 eggs
½ cup butter
1 tablespoon Marsala or any sweet
   wine
1 teaspoon salt
¼ lb calf's brains
¼ lb calf's brains
¼ cup lard or bacon fat
½ onion
1 small carrot
½ lb chicken giblets
6 tablespoons dry white wine
1 tablespoon tomato sauce
½ cup stock
salt and pepper
1¼ cups milk
grated nutmeg
1 cup grated parmesan cheese

Make a dough with 2¼ cups (9 oz) of the flour, the durum wheat flour, eggs, 2 tablespoons (1 oz) butter, the Marsala and a level teaspoon salt. Knead well until smooth and elastic and roll out fairly thin, then cut into strips about 4in wide with a pastry wheel, and cut them to fit the dish in which you will bake the *vincisgrassi*.

Blanch the sweetbreads and brains in lightly salted boiling water for a few minutes, then remove the outer membrane. Melt the lard and ¼ cup (2 oz) butter and sauté the chopped onion and carrot. When the onion is transparent add the chopped chicken giblets (reserve the liver). Add the white wine and let it evaporate, uncovered, over a good heat until you cannot smell it any longer. Stir in the tomato sauce mixed with a little stock or warm water. Season with salt and freshly ground pepper and cook, covered, over a low heat for about 1 hour, stirring occasionally and adding some of the milk. About 20 minutes before it is ready add the diced sweetbreads, brain and liver.

Cook the pasta in plenty of boiling salted water for half the cooking time – about 2 minutes if it is fresh; drain under cold water and lay out to dry on a cloth.

Make *béchamel* sauce: heat 2 tablespoons butter (1oz) until it foams, then stir in 2 tablespoons flour. Cook until golden, then stir in one cup (½ pint) warm (not boiling) milk, stirring so that it does not burn. Season with salt and freshly ground white pepper and a little grated nutmeg to taste. Simmer for 15–20 minutes, stirring occasionally to obtain a smooth, creamy sauce. It is best used immediately, but if it gets cold and lumpy just stir over a low heat until smooth.

Grease an ovenproof dish and put in alternate layers of pasta, covered with some *béchamel* and grated parmesan, then the meat sauce, ending with a layer of *béchamel*. Leave to stand in a cool place then cook in a moderate oven for about 30 minutes until golden brown. Pour over a little melted butter and serve immediately.

This is a recipe from the area around Macerata. Sometimes ground (minced) veal is used instead of sweetbreads and brains, and sometimes ¾ cup (1oz) dried mushrooms (previously soaked for half an hour in warm water) are added to the meat sauce.

Serves 4

Maccheronci alla pesarese · MACARONI WITH VEAL AND CHICKEN LIVERS   (the Marches)

1 small onion
$\frac{1}{4}$lb lean veal
$\frac{1}{2}$ cup butter
1 cup stock
salt and pepper
$\frac{1}{4}$lb chicken livers
1 black truffle
$\frac{1}{4}$lb cooked ham, chopped
1 cup cream
$\frac{3}{4}$lb macaroni large enough to be
   filled
1$\frac{1}{3}$ cups grated parmesan cheese

Chop well the onion and veal. Melt 3 tablespoons (1$\frac{1}{2}$ oz) butter and cook the chopped mixture over a moderate heat, stirring continually, then add the stock and season with salt and freshly ground pepper. Cook uncovered for about 30 minutes over a low heat, stirring from time to time. Put the chicken livers through a food mill. Clean and finely chop the truffle; chop the ham. Put in a bowl with the chicken livers and work together with a wooden spoon, then season with salt and freshly ground black pepper, gradually adding about two-thirds of the cream to obtain a smooth, but not too thick filling.

Cook the macaroni in plenty of boiling salted water until half done, then put in cold water and drain well. Leave to dry on a cloth then use a special syringe or a pastry bag to stuff the macaroni with the filling. Arrange a layer in the bottom of a broad, buttered ovenproof dish; pour over some of the meat sauce, sprinkle with grated parmesan and make a second layer of stuffed macaroni. Pour over more sauce and sprinkle with parmesan. Cover with the remaining cream, dot with butter and cook in a low oven for about 15 minutes until golden brown. Serve very hot.

Serves 4

Above: maccheroni alla pesarese

Gnocchi al sugo di papera · GNOCCHI WITH DUCK SAUCE   (the Marches)

5 to 6 medium potatoes
2 eggs
salt and pepper
2$\frac{1}{4}$ cups (sifted) flour
4 tablespoons olive oil
1 medium onion
1 sprig parsley
1 duck cut in small serving pieces
6 tablespoons dry white wine
1$\frac{1}{2}$ cups canned (tinned) peeled
   tomatoes
$\frac{2}{3}$ cup grated parmesan cheese

This is a traditional dish from the Marches, where duck is called *papera* instead of the normal Italian term, *anitra*. Make the *gnocchi*: boil the potatoes, peel and put through a food mill or potato ricer, then mix with the eggs, a pinch of salt and the flour, as in *gnocchi con ragù di carne*, page 153. Heat the oil and cook the finely chopped onion and parsley until the onion is transparent. Roll the duck pieces in flour and brown on all sides in the pan with the onion. Raise the heat and add the white wine, then let it evaporate uncovered until the smell is gone. Put the tomatoes through a food mill and add to the pan. Season with salt and freshly ground pepper, bring to a boil, then lower the heat and cook, covered, stirring occasionally to prevent the sauce from burning, until the duck is tender.

Cook the *gnocchi* in plenty of boiling salted water, drain and serve with a few tablespoons of duck sauce and some pieces of duck on each helping. Serve grated parmesan separately. Any remaining duck can be served as a second course.

Serves 4

Below: gnocchi al sugo di papera

Tagliolini alla marinara · TAGLIOLINI WITH FISH   (the Marches)

2¾ cups (sifted) flour
3 eggs
1 teaspoon grated lemon rind (peel)
2lb fillet of cod, haddock, flounder,
 etc.
4 tablespoons oil
1 clove garlic
1 sprig parsley
1 tablespoon tomato sauce
salt and pepper

Make a firm dough with the flour, eggs and 1 teaspoon grated lemon rind (peel). Roll out very thinly, leave to dry a little, then roll up and cut into very thin strips or *tagliolini* (see photograph).

Make a fish stock: clean the fish leaving the heads on, then put in a fish kettle with water to cover and a little salt and boil for about 15 minutes. Heat the oil in a pan, add the garlic and half the finely chopped parsley. Sieve the fish well and press the heads to get out all the flavour, then add to the pan with the tomato sauce. Season with salt and freshly ground pepper and cook over a low heat until the sauce is reduced but still fairly liquid.

Cook the *tagliolini* in plenty of boiling salted water, drain well and mix with the fish stock. Serve very hot sprinkled with the remaining parsley – chopped at the very last minute, or it loses a lot of its flavour. No cheese is served with this dish.

The fish can be filleted, seasoned with salt and pepper, a little oil and some chopped parsley, and served as a second course with lemon quarters and boiled potatoes.

Serves 4

Maccheroncelli alla campofilone · MACCHERONCELLI WITH MEAT (the Marches)

2¾ cups (sifted) flour
3 eggs
½ cup butter
½lb lean veal
½lb loin of pork
5 large ripe or canned (tinned)
  peeled tomatoes
salt and pepper
stock (optional)
¼lb chicken livers or giblets
pecorino cheese

Make a pasta dough with the flour and eggs and knead until smooth and elastic. Roll out very thin, let dry a little, then roll up and cut into very fine *maccheroncelli* – almost as thin as *capelli d'angelo*. Melt the butter and brown the veal and pork on all sides over a moderate heat, then add the tomatoes, after putting through a food mill. Season with salt and freshly ground pepper and cook over a low heat for about 1½ hours. If the sauce thickens too much add a few tablespoons hot stock (or just water). Just before it is ready remove the pork and veal and add the very finely chopped chicken livers or giblets.

Cook the *maccheroncelli* in plenty of boiling salted water for under a minute, then put in a hot serving dish with the meat sauce. Sprinkle with grated *pecorino*, (or use parmesan if you prefer a less piquant flavour). Serve the pork and veal sliced as a second course with a green salad or radishes.

Serves 4

Gnocchi alla romana · GNOCCHI WITH BUTTER AND CHEESE

(Latium)

$6\frac{1}{4}$ cups milk
full 1 cup fine ground farina
2 egg yolks
$\frac{1}{2}$ cup butter
1 cup grated parmesan cheese

Boil the milk in a medium pan and slowly add the farina, stirring continually with a wooden spoon so it does not burn. Every now and then stop adding farina and beat the mixture hard. It should be fairly runny to start with; leave to cook without stirring for 20 minutes and remove from the heat. Beat the egg yolks in a bowl and add a few tablespoons of milk. Beat $\frac{1}{4}$ cup (2oz) butter into the farina before it cools and then add the egg mixture beating vigorously so that the eggs don't cook. Wet a large flat dish or a piece of aluminium foil and pour in the mixture. Leave at least 2 hours.

Turn on to a pastry board or working surface, and cut into rounds with a pastry cutter or the rim of a thin glass. Arrange attractively in a greased ovenproof dish (see photograph). If you need to make more than one layer separate the layers with part of the $\frac{1}{4}$ cup (2oz) butter and grated cheese. Pour melted butter over the top and bake in a medium oven until golden brown. Sprinkle with grated cheese and serve very hot.

Serves 4

Above: gnocchi alla romana

Rigatoni con la pagliata · RIGATONI WITH CHITTERLINGS

(Latium)

$\frac{1}{2}$lb *rigatoni*
$1\frac{1}{4}$lb calf's or beef duodenum
1 medium onion
1 small stick celery
1 clove garlic
1 sprig parsley
$\frac{1}{2}$ cup Canadian (unsmoked) bacon or
    Italian *pancetta*, chopped
4 tablespoons olive oil
6 tablespoons dry white wine
$1\frac{3}{4}$ cups canned (tinned) peeled
    tomatoes
salt and pepper
nutmeg
$\frac{1}{2}$ cup grated *pecorino* cheese

Pagliata is the part of beef or calf's intestine known as the duodenum, which is still full of chyme. Calf's duodenum is very tender, but beef duodenum has a better flavour. Use a knife to remove the hard outer membrane and cut into pieces about 10 in long. Remove as much fat as possible, then use white kitchen thread to sew the outside edges together to make rings (see photograph).

Finely chop the onion, celery, garlic, parsley and bacon. Put the oil in a pan, preferably an earthenware casserole, and cook the chopped vegetables and bacon over a moderate heat until the onion is soft. Add the *pagliata* and brown on all sides; raise the heat and moisten with the white wine. Let it evaporate until the smell has disappeared, then add the tomatoes, which have been put through a food mill. Season with salt and freshly ground pepper and grated nutmeg to taste and cook, covered, over a very low heat for about 3 hours, stirring occasionally. Add a little warm water if it seems too dry. Cook the pasta in plenty of boiling salted water, drain and put in a deep serving dish with the *pagliata*, the sauce and the grated *pecorino*. Mix well and arrange the *pagliata* on top; serve immediately.

Serves 4

Below: rigatoni con la pagliata

Pasta e broccoli · PASTA WITH BROCCOLI (Latium)

1 broccoli or cauliflower
2 anchovy fillets
3 tablespoons olive oil
½ cup raw prosciutto, chopped
1 small onion
1 clove garlic
1 sprig parsley
6 tablespoons dry white wine
1½ cups canned (tinned) peeled
 tomatoes
salt
stock
¾lb pasta (*penne*, *nocciole*, macaroni,
 etc.)
grated parmesan cheese (optional)

Remove the florets from the cauliflower, leaving the stalks intact. Wash the anchovies and chop well. Heat the oil and lightly brown the chopped prosciutto, onion, garlic and parsley, then add the anchovies, the wine and the tomatoes, which have been put through a food mill. Season with salt and simmer for about 15 minutes. Add the cauliflower florets and cook for a further 5 or 6 minutes, then add about 1¼ cups (½ pint) stock and the pasta. Cook until the pasta is still nice and firm, adding more hot stock as necessary. Put in a serving dish, sprinkle with grated cheese if desired.

The raw prosciutto can be sliced thin and added at the last moment so its flavour is more noticeable.

Serves 4

Above : pasta e broccoli

Spaghetti cacio e pepe · SPAGHETTI WITH CHEESE AND PEPPER (Latium)

¾lb spaghetti
salt
plenty of black pepper
¾ cup grated *pecorino* cheese

Cook the spaghetti in plenty of boiling salted water and drain, reserving a few tablespoons of the water, then put the pasta in a deep serving bowl. Grind over lots of pepper, sprinkle with grated *pecorino* and the hot spaghetti cooking water to melt the cheese into a lovely creamy sauce. Mix well and serve very hot.

It is claimed that this is an invention of shepherds in ancient Latium and the Abruzzi. It is far less piquant than it may seem from the description.

Serves 4

Bucatini all'amatriciana · BUCATINI WITH PANCETTA, HOT PEPPER AND TOMATO (Latium)

3 firm tomatoes
1 cup Italian *pancetta* or bacon, diced
1 tablespoon olive oil
1 tablespoon onion, finely chopped
½ piece hot chili pepper
salt
¾lb *bucatini*
½ cup grated *pecorino* cheese

This should not be just another version of tomato sauce; the *pancetta* is added at the last moment so it is crisp and delicious, and the tomato flavour is very light. To obtain this result the diced bacon must be kept hot while the tomato sauce is being prepared. Plunge the tomatoes in boiling water and remove the skins, then squeeze out the seeds, cut in slices and leave to drain. Brown the *pancetta* in the oil over a low heat until crisp, then remove from the oil and reserve. Add the chopped onion and hot pepper to the oil and when the onion is golden add the tomato and a little salt.

Take off the fire and add the cubes of bacon. Cook the *bucatini* in plenty of boiling salted water, drain and put in a hot serving dish with the sauce and sprinkle with grated *pecorino*. Mix well and serve very hot.

Serves 4

Below : bucatini all'amatriciana

Fettuccine al triplo burro maestose · FETTUCCINE TRIPLE BUTTER (Latium)

2¾ **cups (sifted) flour**
3 eggs
1⅓ **cups grated parmesan cheese**
½ **cup butter**

Make a dough with the flour, eggs and a pinch of salt and knead until smooth and elastic (you should hear the air bubbles pop when you cut it). Leave to stand covered with a damp cloth for a few minutes, then roll out not too thinly, leave to dry a little and cut in strips ⅜in wide. Cook the fresh pasta in plenty of boiling salted water for just about 50 seconds; it should be firm, but not too firm. (If using commercially made pasta, cooking time is longer — about 4 minutes, or to taste.) Put in a deep serving dish with the grated parmesan and gradually add the butter in small pieces (it is double or triple butter depending on the amount you use, but it should always be a lot). Serve on very hot plates.

Fettuccine are particularly nice prepared in this way, as they absorb all the butter without losing their lightness and delicacy. Remember that in any recipe where pasta is mixed with butter and cheese the cheese should be added first.

Serves 4

Frittata di spaghetti · SPAGHETTI OMELET   (Latium)

¾lb spaghetti
3 tablespoons butter, melted
1 cup grated parmesan cheese
2 eggs
salt and pepper
1 sprig parsley
2–3 tablespoons olive oil

This is an economical recipe for using up leftover pasta, even if it has already been mixed with butter or tomato sauce. If you haven't any leftover pasta cook fresh spaghetti in plenty of boiling salted water, drain and mix with the melted butter and ½ cup (1½oz) grated parmesan. Leave to cool completely, stirring frequently with a fork so it does not stick together. When cold mix in the beaten eggs, the remaining parmesan, a little freshly ground pepper and the finely chopped parsley. Mix carefully, thoroughly but gently. Put 2 tablespoons oil in a big frying pan (preferably cast iron) and when it is hot pour in the spaghetti and shape it into a sort of omelet. Cook over a moderate heat. Try to get the omelet to brown evenly by turning it round in the pan, always in the same direction. When one side is brown slide it on to a plate and return to the pan to brown the other side, adding another tablespoon of oil. Leave to cool slightly before serving as this gives it a better flavour.

Serves 4

**scant 2 cups very finely ground
durum wheat flour**
4 eggs
salt and pepper
$\frac{1}{4}$ cup butter
$\frac{1}{2}$ cup bacon, chopped
**4 very ripe tomatoes, skinned and
seeded**
$\frac{1}{2}$ cup grated *pecorino* cheese

This traditional recipe from the Abruzzi calls for pure durum wheat flour and of course the *chitarra*, or "guitar" — a wooden guitar-shaped frame with steel strings set about $\frac{1}{8}$in apart on it. Make a pasta dough with the flour, eggs and a pinch of salt. Knead very well until smooth and elastic. Roll out not too thin (it should be about $\frac{1}{8}$in thick, like the distance between the "strings" of the guitar. Cut in rectangles the length and breadth of the "guitar" and press down one piece of dough at a time with the rolling pin so the wires cut the pasta into four-cornered strands of spaghetti. If you have no "guitar" just feed the pasta dough through a pasta machine in fairly thick sheets, using the roller setting for thin *tagliatelle*. The success of this pasta really depends on long and patient kneading of the dough. Cook the macaroni in plenty of boiling salted water until still quite firm and drain.

This is one of the best sorts of fresh pasta and only needs a simple sauce with it such as the following: heat $\frac{1}{4}$ cup (2 oz) butter and fry 2 oz bacon cut in thin strips, then add skinned, seeded tomatoes and cook until you have a thick sauce. Serve with grated *pecorino* and a little pepper.

Serves 4

6 eggs
1¾ cups, sliced *mozzarella* cheese
5 tablespoons butter
1½ cups ground (minced) lean veal
4 tablespoons dry white wine
1½ cups canned (tinned) peeled
** tomatoes, puréed in a food mill**
1 tablespoon concentrated tomato
** paste (purée)**
salt and pepper
1⅓ cups grated parmesan cheese
2¾ cups (sifted) flour

Hard-boil 2 of the eggs and dice them coarsely. Similarly dice the *mozzarella*. Heat 1 tablespoon (½ oz) butter and when it starts to foam add the ground (minced) veal and brown thoroughly, then moisten with the wine and let it cook rapidly until you can't smell the wine any more. Add the puréed tomatoes and the concentrated tomato paste (purée) and bring to a boil. Season with salt and pepper. Reduce heat and let simmer. Mix 3 tablespoons parmesan and 1 egg in a bowl then stir this gradually into the meat sauce. Cook over a low heat until thick.

Make a pasta dough with 3 eggs and the flour and knead until smooth and elastic, then roll out thin and cut into strips the same width as the dish you will bake the *lasagne* in. Cook the fresh pasta for 1 minute in boiling salted water (for commercial pasta, follow package directions), drain and put carefully on a cloth to dry. Grease an ovenproof dish and cover the bottom and sides with the largest strips of pasta. Cover with meat sauce, then sprinkle evenly with the diced hard-boiled egg and *mozzarella*. Cover with another layer of pasta and continue in this way, ending with a layer of pasta. Pour over some melted butter and bake in a moderate oven for about 15 minutes. Serve very hot.

Serves 4

Fusilli alla napoletana · FUSILLI WITH TOMATO AND CHEESE

(Campania)

1 medium onion
1 stalk celery
1 small carrot
1 clove garlic
½ cup Canadian (unsmoked) bacon, sliced thin
1 cup diced *mozzarella* cheese
3 tablespoons olive oil
6 tablespoons dry white wine
4 ripe or canned (tinned) peeled tomatoes
1 tablespoon concentrated tomato paste (purée)
salt and pepper
¾lb *fusilli*
⅔ cup grated *pecorino* cheese
1 pinch oregano

Chop the onion, celery, carrot and garlic into very narrow strips. Slice the bacon and dice the *mozzarella*. Heat the oil in a big pan and lightly brown the chopped vegetables and bacon, then add the wine and let it evaporate over a good heat. Stir in the peeled, seeded tomatoes (or canned (tinned) tomatoes put through a food mill), and the concentrated tomato paste (purée). Season with salt and pepper, lower the heat and cook until thick, stirring occasionally.

Cook the *fusilli* in plenty of boiling salted water; drain while still firm and mix with the other ingredients in the pan and 1 tablespoon grated *pecorino*. If the sauce is too thick dilute with a few tablespoons of the pasta cooking water. Let the pasta absorb all the flavour until it is *al dente*, then put in a hot serving dish and cover with the diced *mozzarella*, sprinkle with oregano and serve immediately. Serve the remaining *pecorino* separately. Alternatively, use fresh *ricotta* instead of *mozzarella*.

Serves 4

Above left and right: fusilli; fusilli alla napoletana

Spaghetti aglio e olio · SPAGHETTI WITH GARLIC AND OIL

(Campania)

¾lb spaghetti
4 tablespoons very good olive oil
4 cloves garlic
1 sprig parsley
salt and pepper

Cook the spaghetti in plenty of boiling salted water. Heat the oil and sauté the crushed cloves of garlic until golden, then remove from the pan. Keep heating the oil. Chop the parsley fine. Drain the pasta while still quite firm, sprinkle with freshly ground black pepper and pour the very hot oil and a sprig of parsley over it. Mix well and serve very hot with a sprig of parsley on top.

For a stronger flavour cook a little bit of hot chili pepper in the oil with the garlic and remove it at the same time as the garlic.

Serves 4

Below left: spaghetti aglio e olio

Spaghetti al pomodoro e basilico · SPAGHETTI WITH TOMATO AND BASIL

(Campania)

6 large firm ripe tomatoes
4 tablespoons olive oil
1 sprig fresh basil
salt and pepper
¾lb spaghetti or *vermicelli*
½ cup grated *pecorino* or parmesan cheese

Make this simple, appetizing sauce: plunge the tomatoes in boiling water and remove the skins, squeeze out the seeds and cut in strips, then leave to drain. Heat the oil and add the tomatoes, basil and some salt and pepper, then cook over a moderate heat for about 30 minutes. When the sauce is thick remove the basil. Stir occasionally so it does not burn. Cook the pasta in plenty of boiling salted water, drain while still firm and mix with the sauce. Serve grated *pecorino* or parmesan separately.

Serves 4

Below right: spaghetti al pomodoro e basilico

Strangulaprievete · "PRIEST-CHOKERS"

3 or 4 medium potatoes
2¼ cups (sifted) flour
1 teaspoon salt
3 tablespoons oil
4 large ripe or canned (tinned)
   peeled tomatoes
salt and pepper
several basil leaves
1 cup grated parmesan cheese

Neapolitan *strangulaprievete* are a sort of flour and potato *gnocchi*, unlike the far more ancient *strangulaprenti*, from Lucano, which are made with flour and boiling water, although the final shape is the same.

Cook the potatoes, remove the skins and while still hot put through a potato ricer on to a pastry board or working surface. Gradually mix in the flour and 1 level teaspoon salt and knead well until smooth and elastic, but not at all sticky (if the dough is too soft add a little more flour). Make into small pieces about 1 in long, cut these into smaller pieces and press each piece down on the floured pastry board with your thumb to give them the traditional *gnocchi* shape. Leave to rest on a floured cloth well apart for about 15 minutes.

Make a simple sauce: heat the oil with the peeled, seeded fresh tomatoes (or puréed canned (tinned) tomatoes) and season with salt and freshly ground pepper and a few basil leaves. Cook over a low heat until thick. Meanwhile cook the *strangulaprievete* in plenty of boiling salted water and remove with a slotted spoon as they come to the surface. Put on very hot plates and serve with the sauce; serve grated parmesan separately.

Serves 4

Spaghetti alle vongole · SPAGHETTI WITH CLAMS

(Campania)

4 large ripe or canned (tinned)
  peeled tomatoes
2 cloves garlic
1 sprig parsley
3 tablespoons olive oil
1¼lb fresh or canned (tinned) clams
  in their own juice
salt and pepper
¾lb spaghetti

If you use fresh clams, wash well, put in a pan with water 1½in deep and bring to a lively boil. When clams open, remove with a slotted spoon. When cool remove from shells. Reserve the liquid, allow to settle and filter through a cloth. Plunge the tomatoes in boiling water and remove the skins, and put through a food mill. Chop very fine the garlic and half the parsley. Heat the oil with the juice from the clams in the can (or from the fresh clams), and the chopped garlic and parsley, season with salt and cook down until there are only a few spoonfuls of liquid left in the pan. Add freshly ground pepper and the clams; do not let them boil but make sure they are very hot.

Cook the spaghetti in plenty of boiling salted water, drain and put in a serving dish with the clams and the remaining chopped parsley (chop it right at the last minute or it loses a lot of its flavour). Grated cheese is not served with this dish.

It makes a more digestible dish if you add the oil to the spaghetti in the serving dish instead of cooking it with the garlic and parsley.

Serves 4

Spaghetti con le cozze · SPAGHETTI WITH MUSSELS (Campania)

2qt mussels
¾lb spaghetti
4 tablespoons olive oil
2 tablespoons parsley
2 cloves garlic
salt and pepper
lemon rind (peel)

Scrub the mussels with a hard brush until very clean, then put in a pan with about 6 tablespoons water and cook over a good heat. Remove from the pan as they open, discard the shells and wash in warm water so they are completely free from sand. Reserve their cooking liquid: leave it to stand so the sand goes to the bottom, then put the liquid through a very fine sieve or a piece of gauze.

Cook the spaghetti in plenty of boiling salted water. Put the oil and finely chopped garlic in a pan and pour in the mussel liquid very slowly so any remaining sand remains in the bowl. Let the liquid evaporate a bit over a good heat, then add the mussels and cook for a few minutes until they change colour. Season with salt and pepper and 1 teaspoon grated lemon rind (peel). Drain the pasta while still firm and put in a deep serving bowl; pour the sauce and the mussels over the pasta and sprinkle with the parsley. Serve immediately. Grated cheese is not usually served with this dish.

Alternatively, sprinkle with a pinch of oregano when adding the parsley.

Serves 4

Above: spaghetti con le cozze

Spaghetti alla marinara · SPAGHETTI WITH TOMATOES AND OLIVES (Campania)

4 tablespoons olive oil
20 black olives
1 tablespoon capers
1 clove garlic
5 large firm ripe or canned (tinned)
   peeled tomatoes
3 basil leaves
¾lb spaghetti
salt

Make the sauce in advance. Put the oil in an enamel or earthenware casserole with the pitted (stoned), chopped olives and finely chopped capers and garlic, the peeled, seeded tomatoes (or canned (tinned) tomatoes put through a food mill) and the basil. Leave to marinate for 30 minutes, then cook over a moderate heat until thick and creamy. Remove the basil and mix in a deep serving bowl with the spaghetti, just drained after being cooked to a chewy firmness in plenty of boiling salted water. Grated cheese is not served with this dish. Alternatively add a little piece of hot chili pepper to the marinade and remove when the sauce is thick.

Serves 4

Below: spaghetti alla marinara

Spaghetti alla pizzaiola · SPAGHETTI WITH TOMATOES · (Campania)

1 clove garlic
4 large ripe or canned (tinned)
  peeled tomatoes
4 tablespoons olive oil
salt and pepper
1 tablespoon capers
¾lb spaghetti
1 pinch oregano
1 sprig parsley
grated *pecorino* cheese (optional)

Chop fine the clove of garlic (remove the centre if you wish to make it more easily digestible). Plunge the tomatoes in boiling water and remove the skins, squeeze out the seeds and cut in thin slices, or put canned (tinned) peeled tomatoes through a food mill. Put the oil, garlic and tomatoes in a pan, season with salt and freshly ground pepper and cook over a good heat until thick, then add the capers and remove from the heat. Cook the spaghetti in plenty of boiling salted water, drain and mix with the sauce, then sprinkle with the oregano and freshly chopped parsley.

This simple but tasty dish is delicious with grated *pecorino*.

Serves 4

Above left: spaghetti alla pizzaiola

Vermicelli alle alici salse · VERMICELLI WITH ANCHOVIES · (Campania)

¾lb *vermicelli*
4 tablespoons olive oil
1 clove garlic
4 salt-cured anchovies or anchovy
  fillets
salt and pepper

Cook the *vermicelli* in plenty of boiling salted water, heat the oil in a large pan and brown the garlic, then discard it. Wash the anchovies and fillet them if necessary, then chop coarsely and crush in the oil with a fork to make a smooth, thick sauce. Drain the pasta and add to the anchovies so it absorbs the flavour over a moderate heat. Season with a little freshly ground pepper and serve immediately.

Serves 4

Above right: vermicelli alle alici salse

Maccheroni alla napoletana di artusi · MACARONI WITH TOMATO SAUCE · (Campania)

1 small onion
1 sprig basil
¼ cup butter
3 or 4 large ripe or canned (tinned)
  peeled tomatoes
salt and pepper
¾lb grooved macaroni
⅔ cup grated parmesan cheese

Finely chop the onion and basil and cook for a few minutes in 2 tablespoons (1oz) butter. Peel the tomatoes, squeeze out the seeds and slice coarsely, or put canned (tinned) tomatoes through a food mill. Season with salt and pepper and simmer until nice and thick. Cook the macaroni in plenty of boiling salted water, drain while still firm and put in a serving dish. Dot with the remaining butter, mix in the sauce and sprinkle with grated parmesan (or *pecorino* for a stronger flavour). Serve very hot.

Serves 4

Below: maccheroni alla napoletana di artusi

Orecchiette al sugo di agnello · ORECCHIETTE WITH LAMB

(Apulia)

full 1 cup durum wheat flour
scant 1 cup (sifted) flour
$\frac{1}{2}$ cup butter
2 tablespoons olive oil
1 sprig rosemary
$2\frac{1}{4}$lb boned lean lamb, leg or shoulder
salt and pepper
$\frac{2}{3}$ cup grated parmesan cheese

Mix the durum wheat flour, flour and enough water to make a fairly firm dough. Knead well until smooth and elastic. Make into small pieces about 1 in long, then cut in little bits $\frac{1}{4}$ in long and press them with your thumb against the table to obtain the traditional concave caps with a ribbed outside. Leave to dry for at least a day.

Heat the butter and oil in a pan with the rosemary, then brown the lamb on all sides over a low heat with the lid on. Season with salt and freshly ground pepper and cook gently adding a few tablespoons water as necessary until the meat is tender, then remove the rosemary. Cook the *orecchiette* in plenty of boiling salted water, drain and put in a deep serving dish with the lovely thick dark coloured sauce from the lamb. Serve with grated parmesan. Serve the lamb as a second course with a green salad.

Serves 4

Orecchiette con il ragù · ORECCHIETTE WITH MEAT SAUCE (Apulia)

1 medium onion
1 stalk celery
4 or 5 basil leaves
4 tablespoons olive oil
¾lb ground (minced) beef
1½ cups canned (tinned) peeled
   tomatoes
salt and pepper
¾lb *orecchiette*
⅔ cup grated parmesan cheese

Chop the onion, celery and basil and cook in the oil over a moderate heat, then add the ground (minced) beef. Raise the heat a little and brown lightly throughout. Put the tomatoes through a food mill and add to the meat, then season with salt and freshly ground pepper, cover and cook until thick. Cook the *orecchiette* (you can make them as in *Orecchiette al sugo di agnello*, page 108) in plenty of boiling salted water until done (always slightly *al dente*), drain and mix with the meat sauce, sprinkle with grated parmesan and serve very hot.

This is a delicious and economical sauce.

Serves 4

Orecchiette con le cime di rapa strascicate · ORECCHIETTE WITH FRIED TURNIP TOPS (Apulia)

¾lb *orecchiette*
¾lb turnip tops
4 tablespoons olive oil
pinch hot chili pepper
1 clove garlic
salt

Make the *orecchiette* as in *orecchiette al sugo di agnello*, page 108, or use commercial *orecchiette*. Wash the turnip tops and cook in plenty of boiling salted water until tender but still firm and green. Drain and reserve the cooking water. Heat the oil with the chili pepper and finely chopped garlic, add the turnip tops and salt to taste and leave to cook a little. Remove the chili pepper when the taste is at the desired strength. Cook the *orecchiette* in the vegetable cooking water and drain while still firm, then add to the pan. Mix with the turnip tops and serve very hot.

This is usually not served with grated cheese.

Serves 4

Above left : orecchiette con le cime di rapa strascicate

Orecchiette col pomodoro e la ricotta · ORECCHIETTE WITH TOMATOES AND RICOTTA (Apulia)

¾lb *orecchiette*
3 large ripe or the equivalent canned (tinned) peeled tomatoes
salt and pepper
¾ cup *ricotta* cheese

Use commercial *orecchiette*, or make them fresh as in *orecchiette al sugo di agnello*, page 108. Cook them in plenty of boiling salted water. Put the tomatoes through a food mill and heat the purée over a good heat until thick and creamy, then season with salt and pepper and remove from the heat. Mash the *ricotta* with a fork and mix with the tomato purée. Drain the pasta and put in a deep serving bowl, add freshly ground pepper and the sauce, mix well and serve very hot.

Serves 4

Above right : orecchiette col pomodoro e la ricotta

Spaghetti con i broccoli · SPAGHETTI WITH BROCCOLI (Apulia)

4 anchovy fillets or salt-cured anchovies
1¾lb broccoli florets
salt
¾lb spaghetti
4 tablespoons olive oil
1 clove garlic, finely chopped

Wash the anchovies, fillet if necessary and chop coarsely. Cut off any coarse parts of the stem from the broccoli florets, wash well and cook until only just tender in boiling salted water. Drain and reserve the cooking water for the spaghetti. While the pasta is cooking in this water heat the oil with the finely chopped garlic and the anchovies, mashing the anchovies with a fork to make a thick sauce. Drain the spaghetti and put in a deep serving bowl, then mix with the anchovy sauce and broccoli. Serve at once.

Grated cheese is not usually served with this dish. For a more spicy flavour add a little bit of finely chopped hot chili pepper to the oil.

Serves 4

Below : spaghetti con i broccoli

$\frac{3}{4}$–1 lb cuttlefish or squid
1 small onion
1 stalk celery
1 clove garlic
1 small carrot
4 tablespoons olive oil
salt and pepper
6 tablespoons dry white wine
2 cups stock
1 sprig parsley
$\frac{3}{4}$ lb spaghetti

Clean the cuttlefish or squid, removing the eyes, mouth, central bone, intestines and ink sack. Cut the tentacles and body in thin slices. Or purchase already cleaned or canned. Chop fine the onion, celery, garlic and carrot and cook in the oil until soft, then add the cuttlefish or squid and cook for a few minutes with some salt and freshly ground pepper over a moderate heat. Moisten with the wine, let it evaporate uncovered until the smell has disappeared, then cook for about one hour, until tender, adding a little hot stock or a bouillon cube and hot water, from time to time as the liquid dries out. When nearly ready add the chopped parsley. Cook the spaghetti in plenty of boiling salted water, drain while still firm and put in a hot serving dish with the squid sauce. No cheese is served with this dish.

Alternatively, you can omit the wine and stock and add either 4 large tomatoes skinned and put through a food mill, or 1$\frac{3}{4}$ cups (14 oz) canned (tinned) peeled tomatoes.

Serves 4

5 large ripe or canned (tinned) peeled tomatoes
3 anchovy fillets or salt-cured anchovies
4 tablespoons olive oil
1 clove garlic
3 basil leaves
1 small piece hot chili pepper
¾ lb spaghetti
salt
1 sprig parsley
1 tablespoon capers, chopped (optional)
12 black olives, pitted (stoned) (optional)

Plunge the tomatoes in boiling water and remove the skin, squeeze out the seeds and break the tomatoes with your hands, or put canned (tinned) tomatoes through a food mill. Wash the anchovies and fillet if necessary, then chop coarsely. Heat the anchovies in the oil over a low heat, mashing with a fork so they make a thick sauce. Add the chopped garlic and basil and hot chili pepper, then simmer over a moderate heat until thick, but not too dry. Remove the chili pepper when the sauce is hot enough for your taste. Cook the spaghetti in plenty of boiling salted water; drain when half cooked and mix with the sauce. Raise the heat and finish cooking the spaghetti, stirring all the time. If it seems too dry add a few tablespoons of the pasta cooking water. When it is nearly done add the coarsely chopped parsley and serve very hot. Grated cheese is not usually served with this dish.

If you like, you can add 1 tablespoon chopped capers and 12 pitted (stoned) black olives with the parsley at the end.

Serves 4

Spaghetti alla tarantina · SPAGHETTI WITH SEAFOOD   (Apulia)

$\frac{1}{2}$lb shrimp or prawns
$\frac{3}{4}$lb clams
$\frac{1}{2}$lb (1 pint) mussels
1 clove garlic
4 tablespoons olive oil
$\frac{1}{4}$lb eel, skinned and chopped
salt and pepper
3 large ripe or canned (tinned)
   peeled tomatoes
1 sprig parsley
$\frac{3}{4}$lb spaghetti

Scrub the shellfish shells until very clean then cook with very little water over a good heat. Take mussels and clams from the pan as the shells open. Discard the shells and wash the mussels in warm water to remove all the sand. Leave the cooking liquid to stand so any more sand settles on the bottom, then put it through a very fine sieve or piece of gauze. Wash the shrimp and remove the shells. Brown the garlic in the oil, lower the flame and add the mussels, shrimp, and the skinned, chopped eel. Season with salt and freshly ground pepper, then add the skinned, seeded tomatoes cut in strips (or canned (tinned) peeled tomatoes put through a food mill), together with the mussel liquid. Cook until the eel is tender over a moderate heat. When nearly done add the chopped parsley. Cook the spaghetti in plenty of boiling salted water, drain while still firm and put in a hot serving bowl with the seafood sauce.

Serves 4

114

Lasagna imbottita · STUFFED LASAGNE
(Calabria)

$\frac{3}{4}$ **cup dried mushrooms**
$2\frac{3}{4}$ **cups (sifted) flour**
salt
1lb loin of pork
1 egg
$\frac{1}{4}$ **cup grated *pecorino* cheese**
salt and pepper
olive oil
2 hard-boiled eggs
$\frac{2}{3}$ **cup *mozzarella*, diced**
1 small onion
1 stalk celery
1 small carrot
$1\frac{1}{4}$ **cups fresh shelled peas**

Soak the mushrooms in warm water for about half an hour. Make a dough with the flour, a little salt and some warm water. Knead well and roll out quite thickly, then cut into broad strips about $4\frac{1}{2}$ in wide and the length of the dish you will bake them in. Cut 4 nice slices from the loin of pork and put the rest through a meat grinder (mincer). Mix 1 egg, $\frac{1}{4}$ cup (1oz) *pecorino* and the ground (minced) pork with some salt and pepper in a bowl, then make into small walnut-sized balls and fry them in very hot oil. Slice the hard-boiled eggs and dice the *mozzarella*. Fry the pork slices in the very hot oil. Chop fine the onion, celery and carrot. Heat 2 more tablespoons oil and brown the chopped vegetables and chopped mushrooms, then add the peas and cook covered with a little water until the peas and mushrooms are done.

Cook the fresh *lasagne* in plenty of boiling salted water for only a few seconds. Remove very gently from the pan and leave to drain on a cloth. Grease an ovenproof dish and put in a layer of *lasagne*, and cover with the chopped egg, *mozzarella* and a few meatballs. Put the fried pork slices on the middle layer, pour over half the sauce and add some grated *pecorino*. Make a final layer of pasta, cover with the remaining sauce and grated *pecorino* and bake in a moderate oven for about 30 minutes. Serve very hot.

This is a delicious and substantial dish, best served as the main course.

Serves 4

Spaghetti con i polpi e i totani · SPAGHETTI WITH OCTOPUS AND CUTTLEFISH   (Calabria)

½lb octopus or squid
½lb cuttlefish
1 medium onion
2 cloves garlic
4 tablespoons olive oil
1¾ cups canned (tinned) peeled
  tomatoes
salt and pepper
¾lb spaghetti

You can use squid alone instead of cuttlefish and octopus – double the quantity. Clean well, removing the inside bone, eyes, mouth, intestines and ink sack, and slice in thin rings. Chop the onion and garlic and brown in the oil with the seafood over a low heat. Put the tomatoes through a food mill and add to the seafood mixture, season with salt and simmer over a moderate heat for about an hour, adding warm water if necessary until sauce is thick and the fish is tender. Cook the spaghetti in plenty of boiling salted water, drain while still firm and put in a deep serving dish with the sauce and some freshly ground pepper.

Grated cheese is not served with this dish.

Serves 4

Above left: spaghetti con i polpi e i totani

Pasta coi broccoli "arriminata" · PASTA WITH BROCCOLI AND ANCHOVIES   (Sicily)

2 anchovy fillets or salt-cured
  anchovies
½ cup seedless raisins (sultanas)
1 small cauliflower or broccoli head
5 tablespoons olive oil
1 small onion
1¾ cups canned (tinned) peeled
  tomatoes
salt and pepper
⅓ cup pine nuts (pignoli)
¾lb pasta (macaroni, *mezze maniche*
  or *tortiglioni*)
3 small basil leaves
½ cup grated *pecorino* cheese

Wash the anchovies and fillet if necessary, then chop coarsely. Soak the raisins in warm water for 20 minutes. Cook the cauliflower or broccoli in boiling salted water until tender but still firm, then break off the florets with their tender stalks and reserve. Heat 4 tablespoons olive oil in a casserole and cook the sliced onion until transparent. Put the tomatoes through a food mill then add to the onion in the pan. Add the cauliflower or broccoli, cover the pan and simmer gently. Heat 1 tablespoon olive oil in a small frying pan, add the anchovies and crush them with a fork in the pan to make a smooth, thick sauce. Stir this into the cauliflower or broccoli mixture; check the seasoning, adding a little salt and freshly ground pepper, then the drained raisins and pine nuts and stir until well blended, then leave to stand for a few moments away from the heat. Cook the pasta until still quite firm, drain and put in a deep serving dish with the sauce, some freshly chopped basil and the grated *pecorino*. Serve very hot.

Serves 4

Above right: pasta coi broccoli "arriminata"

Spaghetti con la mollica fritta e l'uva passa ·   (Sicily)
SPAGHETTI WITH FRIED BREAD AND SEEDLESS RAISINS (SULTANAS)

½ cup seedless raisins (sultanas)
¾lb spaghetti
1 clove garlic, crushed
4 tablespoons olive oil
1½ slices stale bread without the crust
1 sprig parsley, chopped
salt and pepper

Soak the raisins (sultanas) in warm water for 30 minutes. Cook the spaghetti in plenty of boiling salted water. Brown the crushed garlic in the oil in a small pan, then discard garlic and add the stale bread, which has been grated into fine crumbs; stir continually, browning throughout. Drain the pasta and mix with the fried breadcrumbs, drained raisins, a little finely chopped parsley and salt and pepper. Mix well and serve very hot.

Grated cheese is not usually served with this dish.

Serves 4

Below: spaghetti con la mollica fritta e l'uva passa

Pasta con le sarde (I) · PASTA WITH SARDINES (I) (Sicily)

2½ tablespoons seedless raisins (sultanas)
2½ tablespoons pine nuts
½lb fresh, filleted sardines
1 medium onion
4 tablespoons olive oil
1 anchovy fillet or salt-cured anchovy
4 large ripe or canned (tinned) peeled tomatoes
salt and pepper
¾lb macaroni, *perciatelli* or *bucatini*

Soak the raisins (sultanas) in warm water for at least 20–30 minutes. Finely chop the pine nuts. Wash the sardines and fillet them, keeping the fillets whole. Cook the chopped onion until transparent in the oil then add the washed (and if necessary filleted) anchovy and cook, mashing it with a fork to make a thick sauce. Put the tomatoes through a food mill and add to the anchovy with the raisins and coarsely chopped pine nuts and leave to simmer for a few minutes. Add the sardine fillets, season with a little salt (check seasoning first as the anchovy is quite salty) and freshly ground pepper, then cook covered over a low heat, stirring from time to time.

Cook the pasta in plenty of boiling salted water, drain while still quite firm then mix in a serving dish with the sardine sauce. Let stand for a few minutes before serving.

Serves 4

Pasta con le sarde (II) · PASTA WITH SARDINES (II) (Sicily)

2½ tablespoons seedless raisins (sultanas)
2½ tablespoons pine nuts
½lb wild fennel (or the green "whiskers" from garden fennel, but the flavour is less delicate)
½lb fresh sardines
1 tablespoon flour
salt and pepper
1 cured anchovy
1 medium onion
olive oil
1 anchovy fillet or salt-cured anchovy
pinch saffron
¾lb macaroni

Soak the raisins (sultanas) in warm water. Toast the pine nuts until light brown in a hot oven. Wash the fennel and put the tender parts only to cook for 10 minutes in plenty of boiling salted water, then drain, reserving the water. Squeeze the fennel to remove the water and chop. Fillet and wash the sardines, but leave the two sides of each fillet joined together. Roll in flour and fry in a little very hot oil over a moderate heat (so they do not get too dried out). Remove from the pan and sprinkle with a little salt. Cook the chopped onion in 4 tablespoons olive oil over a low heat, then add the washed anchovy (filleted if necessary) and crush it in the pan with a fork to make a thick sauce. Add the raisins (sultanas), pine nuts and fennel, a pinch of saffron and a little freshly ground pepper. Mix well and remove from the heat.

Cook the pasta in the fennel cooking water, drain while still firm and put in a deep serving dish with the sauce. Stir in the whole sardine fillets very gently so they do not break. Leave to stand for a few minutes before serving.

This traditional dish from Palermo is not served with grated cheese.

Serves 4

Spaghetti alla Norma · SPAGHETTI WITH EGGPLANT (AUBERGINE) AND TOMATOES (Sicily)

3 eggplants (aubergines)
4 large ripe or canned (tinned)
  peeled tomatoes
8 tablespoons olive oil
1 sprig basil, chopped
2 cloves garlic, crushed
salt and pepper
¾ lb spaghetti
¾ cup grated hard *ricotta* cheese

Cut the eggplants (aubergines) into thin slices, sprinkle with salt and leave in a colander so the bitter juice and excess liquid drains out. Plunge the tomatoes in boiling water to remove the skins, squeeze out the seeds and chop, or put canned (tinned) tomatoes through a food mill. Heat 3 tablespoons olive oil in a pan, add the tomatoes and chopped basil and garlic, season with salt and freshly ground pepper, then cook over a moderate heat until thick. Heat the remaining oil until sizzling, then fry a few slices of eggplant (aubergine) at a time until golden brown, then remove with a fork, put on absorbent kitchen paper and sprinkle with salt and pepper. Cook the spaghetti in plenty of boiling salted water, drain while still firm, put in a serving dish and mix with slices of eggplant (aubergine) and the tomato sauce, then sprinkle with the grated *ricotta*.

This is a highly flavoured dish from Catania named after the colourful native of Catania, Vincenzo Bellini, composer of the famous opera *Norma*.

Serves 4

Above: spaghetti alla Norma

Pasta incaciata · MOULDED PASTA WITH EGGPLANT (AUBERGINE) (Sicily)

2 eggplants (aubergines)
1 hard-boiled egg
⅓ cup *mozzarella* cheese, sliced
1 clove garlic
1 sprig basil
olive oil
5 large ripe or canned (tinned)
  peeled tomatoes
¼ cup ground (minced) lean veal
⅓ cup shelled peas
salt and pepper
2 chicken livers
¾ lb macaroni or *perciatelli*
½ cup grated *pecorino* cheese

Wash the eggplants (aubergines) and cut into thin slices; sprinkle with salt and leave in a colander for at least 30 minutes to drain off the excess juice. Fry slices in very hot oil and drain on absorbent kitchen paper; keep hot. Slice the egg and the *mozzarella*; chop the garlic and basil. Put 4 tablespoons oil in a pan with the chopped basil and garlic, the puréed tomatoes, ground (minced) veal and peas. Season with salt and freshly ground pepper and simmer covered for about 30 minutes. When nearly done add the chopped chicken livers.

Cook the pasta in plenty of boiling salted water and drain while still quite firm. Grease a deep round ovenproof dish (e.g. a soufflé dish) with a little oil, line the sides and bottom with eggplant (aubergine) slices, then fill with half the pasta sprinkled with half the *mozzarella*, the hard-boiled egg and one-third of the tomato sauce. Cover with the remaining pasta, some tomato sauce and the remaining *mozzarella*. Sprinkle with grated *pecorino* and press down to make a firm "cake", then bake in a moderate oven for about 20 minutes. Turn out on to a serving dish and pour over the remaining very hot tomato sauce. Sprinkle with *pecorino* and serve immediately.

If you like a less piquant flavour use parmesan instead of *pecorino*, or use less *pecorino*.

Serves 4

Below: pasta incaciata

Pasta con le melanzane · PASTA WITH EGGPLANT (AUBERGINE) (Sicily)

2 large eggplants (aubergines)
olive oil
1 small piece chili pepper
1 clove garlic, crushed
⅔lb pasta (*vermicelli*, spaghetti,
   perciatelli)
salt
1 sprig parsley, chopped

Peel the eggplants (aubergines) if they seem at all tough, then dice the flesh. Sprinkle with salt and leave in a colander for a couple of hours so the bitter juice drains out. Heat the olive oil with the chili pepper and crushed garlic and when the garlic is brown discard it and fry the diced eggplant (aubergine). Leave the pieces to drain on absorbent kitchen paper. Cook the pasta in plenty of boiling salted water and drain while still firm, then put in a serving dish and mix with a little oil, the chopped parsley and the diced eggplant (aubergine).

No cheese is served with this dish.

Serves 4

Above left: pasta con le melanzane

Pasta con le zucchine · PASTA WITH ZUCCHINI (COURGETTES) (Sicily)

¾lb pasta (spaghetti, *perciatelli, penne*, etc.)
3 large zucchini (courgettes)
4 tablespoons olive oil
salt and pepper

Cook the pasta in plenty of boiling salted water. Wash, dry well and slice the zucchini (courgettes) in thin rounds, then fry in the hot oil with a little salt and freshly ground pepper. Stir frequently so they do not burn. Drain the pasta and put in a serving bowl with the zucchini (courgettes) and their cooking oil. Mix well and serve at once.

Grated cheese is not usually served with this dish.

Serves 4

Opposite page, right : pasta con le zucchine

Vermicelli alla siciliana · VERMICELLI WITH SARDINES (Sicily)

4 ripe tomatoes, peeled
1 tablespoon butter
salt and pepper
4 fresh sardines
5 tablespoons olive oil
¾lb *vermicelli*

Put the tomatoes through a food mill and cook with the butter, a little salt and freshly ground pepper to make a thick sauce. Clean and fillet the sardines and fry 2 of them in 2 tablespoons olive oil, then leave to drain on absorbent kitchen paper, sprinkled with a little salt. Chop the other fillets and cook in the remaining oil in a broad pan with salt and pepper, crushing them with a fork to make a smooth sauce (you can also add 1 tablespoon milk to make it more liquid). Cook the *vermicelli* in plenty of boiling salted water, drain while still firm and add to the sardines in the pan. Mix in the tomato sauce and finish cooking the pasta, stirring continually. Put some whole fried fillets of sardines on each serving of pasta.

This dish usually is not served with grated cheese.

Serves 4

Maccheroncelli con il cavolfiore · MACARONI WITH CAULIFLOWER (Sicily)

1 medium cauliflower
2 anchovy fillets or salt-cured anchovies
1 clove garlic
⅓ cup pine nuts
5 tablespoons olive oil
salt and pepper
¾lb macaroni

Cook the cauliflower in a little salted water (so the florets are not covered). Wash and fillet the anchovies if necessary, and chop together with the garlic and pine nuts, then fry in the oil in a broad pan. Drain the cauliflower while still firm and gently detach the florets and their tender stems. Add to the vegetables in the pan, season with salt and freshly ground pepper, then cook for a few minutes until the cauliflower has absorbed the anchovy flavour. Remove from the heat and keep hot. Cook the macaroni in plenty of boiling salted water and drain while still firm, then mix with the cauliflower. Stir very gently so the pasta absorbs the sauce and the florets remain whole.

Serve very hot : no grated cheese is necessary.

Serves 4

Pasta con la carne capuliata · PASTA WITH MEAT AND TOMATO SAUCE (Sicily)

1 onion
1 clove garlic
1 sprig parsley
2 basil leaves
$\frac{1}{4}$ cup butter
$\frac{3}{4}$lb lean ground (minced) beef
6 tablespoons dry red wine
4 ripe tomatoes
salt and pepper
$\frac{3}{4}$lb pasta (macaroni, spaghetti or
    perciatelli)
$\frac{2}{3}$ cup grated parmesan cheese
$\frac{2}{3}$ cup *caciocavallo* or sharp *provolone*
    cheese, sliced

Chop fine the onion, garlic, parsley and basil. Heat the butter, reserving 1 tablespoon ($\frac{1}{2}$oz), until it foams, then add the chopped vegetables. Cook for a few minutes then add the ground (minced) beef and brown throughout for 3–4 minutes. Raise the heat, moisten the mixture with the wine and let it evaporate, then add the peeled, seeded and chopped tomatoes. Season with salt and freshly ground pepper, cover the pan and cook over a moderate heat for about 30 minutes, stirring occasionally, adding a little hot water.

Cook the pasta in plenty of boiling salted water, drain while still very firm and put in a serving bowl with the meat sauce and grated parmesan. Grease an ovenproof dish with the remaining butter and put in a layer of pasta, slices of *caciocavallo* and then more pasta, ending with a layer of *caciocavallo*. Bake in a moderate oven for about 20 minutes, then serve very hot.

If an even more piquant flavour is desired substitute *pecorino* cheese for parmesan.

Serves 4

Right : pasta con la carne capuliata

Pasta all'aglio e olio del duca · PASTA WITH GARLIC AND OIL (Sicily)

6 cloves garlic
2 tablespoons butter
2 tablespoons flour
$\frac{3}{4}$ cup hot milk
salt and white pepper
$\frac{3}{4}$lb spaghetti
5 tablespoons olive oil

Simmer the garlic cloves in a cup and a half of water over a very low heat for about 2 hours, covered. Make a *béchamel* sauce : melt the butter and when it foams stir in the flour and let it brown for a few seconds, then stir in the hot milk. Season with salt and freshly ground white pepper and simmer for about 20 minutes. Remove from the heat and stir from time to time until needed. Cook the spaghetti in plenty of boiling salted water. Put the garlic with its cooking water through a food mill and return to the pan; add the oil and simmer uncovered to thicken a little. Drain the spaghetti while still firm and put in a serving dish with the *béchamel* and hot garlic sauce. Mix well with two forks so the spaghetti absorbs all the flavour. This sauce does not have the inconvenience of others with a lot of garlic. One may enjoy it without worrying about smelling of garlic.

Serves 4

Pasta a "picchi-pacchi" · PASTA WITH ANCHOVIES AND TOMATOES (Sicily)

3 anchovy fillets or salt-cured
  anchovies
1 large onion
1 clove garlic
1 sprig basil
3 ripe tomatoes
4 tablespoons olive oil
salt and pepper
$\frac{3}{4}$ lb spaghetti

Wash the anchovies and fillet if necessary, then chop coarsely; chop the onion, garlic and basil. Skin the tomatoes, squeeze out the seeds and break the tomatoes in pieces. Slightly brown the chopped vegetables in the oil, then add the anchovies and crush with a fork so they dissolve; finally add the tomatoes. Lower the heat, season with salt and freshly ground pepper and simmer until smooth and thick. Cook the spaghetti in plenty of boiling salted water and mix quickly with the sauce so it can be served very hot.

No grated cheese is served with this dish.

Serves 4

Trionfo della marescialla · SPAGHETTI WITH WINE SAUCE (Sicily)

1 large onion
1 clove garlic
1 sprig parsley
$\frac{1}{4}$ cup butter
1 tablespoon flour
$\frac{3}{4}$ cup dry white wine
1 teaspoon meat extract
salt and pepper
$\frac{3}{4}$ lb spaghetti

Cook the chopped onion, garlic and parsley in the butter and when they start to brown stir in the flour and cook over a good heat until brown. Add the wine and let it evaporate. Lower the heat, moisten with 6 tablespoons warm water and the meat extract, then simmer gently for about 1 hour, stirring occasionally and adding more water as necessary. Season with salt and freshly ground pepper. Cook the spaghetti in plenty of boiling salted water, drain and mix in a deep serving bowl with the sauce.

No grated cheese is served with this dish.

Serves 4

Spaghetti alla siracusana · SPAGHETTI WITH CAPERS AND ANCHOVIES (Sicily)

1 tablespoon salt-cured capers
1 anchovy fillet or salt-cured anchovy
5 tablespoons olive oil
1 clove garlic, crushed
5 large ripe tomatoes
1 sweet yellow pepper, sliced thin
salt and pepper
$\frac{1}{2}$ cup grated *pecorino* cheese
$\frac{3}{4}$ lb spaghetti
3 basil leaves

Wash the capers to remove the salt; chop fine. Wash the anchovy and fillet if necessary, then chop coarsely. Put the oil in a pan with the chopped garlic. Peel the tomatoes, squeeze out the seeds, break into pieces with your hands and add to the oil. Simmer uncovered for about 10 minutes, then add the chopped anchovy, capers and thin-sliced pepper. Season with salt, freshly ground pepper and basil and cook over a moderate heat to obtain a fairly thick sauce.

Cook the spaghetti in plenty of boiling salted water, drain while firm and chewy, place in a hot serving bowl with the anchovy sauce and a little grated *pecorino*. Mix well and serve immediately.

Serves 4

Right: spaghetti alla siracusana

scant 2 cups finely ground durum
   wheat flour
1 onion
1 clove garlic
2 or 3 basil leaves
4 tablespoons olive oil
5 large ripe tomatoes or canned
   (tinned) peeled tomatoes
salt and pepper
1 teaspoon meat extract
pinch saffron
$\frac{1}{2}$ cup grated *pecorino* cheese

Malloreddus are best made 24 hours in advance. Make a pasta dough with the flour, a pinch of salt and a little warm water in which you have dissolved the saffron. Knead very energetically to obtain a smooth, firm dough and roll out, then cut into little strips about the thickness of a pencil, and cut these into $\frac{1}{2}$in pieces. Sprinkle with plenty of flour so they do not stick and press with your thumb against the back of a grater so they look like *gnocchi*. Lay out to dry on a floured cloth. Chop the onion, garlic and basil and brown in the oil, then add the puréed tomatoes. Season with salt and freshly ground pepper, adding the meat extract diluted with 1 tablespoon warm water. Simmer over a moderate heat until the sauce is nice and thick.

Cook the *malloreddus* in plenty of boiling salted water, remove with a slotted spoon as they rise to the surface, then serve with a few tablespoons of the sauce on each helping. Serve the grated *pecorino* separately.

For a richer dish add some ground (minced) meat or sausage meat to the oil and brown before adding the tomatoes.

Serves 4

Maccheroni col ragù · MACARONI WITH MEAT SAUCE (Sardinia)

½lb lean beef (round or chuck)
1 clove garlic
4 tablespoons olive oil
5 large ripe or canned (tinned) peeled
   tomatoes
1 teaspoon meat extract
salt and pepper
1 sprig basil
¾lb macaroni
⅔ cup grated parmesan cheese

Cut the meat into small cubes. Crush the clove of garlic and fry in the olive oil until golden, then remove from the pan. Add the beef and brown on all sides. Plunge the tomatoes in boiling water and remove the skins, squeeze out the seeds gently and add to the oil. Simmer a minute or so, then put in ¾ cup (6 fl oz) hot water with the meat extract dissolved in it. Season with salt, freshly ground pepper and basil and cook uncovered for about 30 minutes over a moderate heat. Cook the macaroni in plenty of boiling salted water, drain while still firm and put in a deep serving bowl with the sauce and some grated parmesan.

For a more piquant flavour use *pecorino* cheese instead of parmesan.

Serves 4

NEW AND FANCIFUL PASTA RECIPES

Spaghetti con i naselli · SPAGHETTI WITH WHITING

$\frac{1}{2}$**lb whiting**
4 tablespoons olive oil
1 small onion
salt and pepper
**1$\frac{1}{2}$ cups canned (tinned) peeled
   tomatoes**
1 sprig parsley
$\frac{3}{4}$**lb spaghetti**

Clean and wash the whiting under cold running water; fillet and chop the flesh into small pieces. Heat the oil and brown the finely chopped onion and the whiting pieces over a moderate heat with some salt and freshly ground pepper. Put the tomatoes through a food mill and add to the fish, then simmer gently until fairly thick. When nearly done add the finely chopped parsley. Cook the spaghetti in plenty of boiling salted water and drain while still firm, then put in a deep serving dish with the fish sauce.

No grated cheese is necessary.

Serves 4

Right: spaghetti con i naselli

Spaghetti alla rustica · SPAGHETTI WITH RUSTIC TOMATO SAUCE

5 large ripe or canned (tinned) peeled
    tomatoes
1 sprig parsley
2 cloves garlic
salt and pepper
¾ lb spaghetti
4 tablespoons olive oil
⅔ cup grated parmesan cheese

Wash the tomatoes and break open with your hands and put in a pan (add canned (tinned) tomatoes directly) with the parsley and crushed cloves of garlic and cook over a moderate heat for about 10 minutes, then put through a food mill. Return to the pan, season with salt and freshly ground pepper and thicken over a low heat. Cook the spaghetti in plenty of boiling salted water and drain while still firm. Put in a hot serving dish with the sauce and uncooked olive oil. Sprinkle with grated parmesan, mix well and serve.

This sauce has a lovely simple flavour that also goes very well with *tagliatelle*.

Serves 4

Above: spaghetti alla rustica

Spaghetti di quaresima · LENTEN SPAGHETTI WITH WALNUTS AND SUGAR

full ½ cup walnuts
⅔ cup dry breadcrumbs
2 tablespoons confectioners (castor)
    sugar
grated nutmeg
salt and pepper
¾ lb spaghetti
4 tablespoons olive oil

Finely chop the walnuts and mix with the breadcrumbs, sugar and some freshly ground pepper and nutmeg to taste. Cook the spaghetti in plenty of boiling salted water, drain while still firm and put in a deep serving dish with the uncooked oil and walnut mixture. Mix well and serve immediately.

Serves 4

Below left: spaghetti di quaresima

Spaghetti con i piselli · SPAGHETTI WITH PEAS

¾ lb spaghetti
½ cup bacon, finely sliced
1¾ cups shelled peas
2 tablespoons olive oil
1 tablespoon butter
1 small onion
1 clove garlic
1 sprig parsley
½ teaspoon meat extract
⅔ cup grated parmesan cheese
salt and pepper

Cut the bacon in thin slices; chop the onion, garlic and parsley. Put the oil in a large pan with the butter and brown the chopped bacon and vegetables over a moderate heat for about 5 minutes, then add the peas and the meat extract dissolved in a little hot water. Cook the spaghetti in boiling salted water. Drain while still quite firm and reserve some of the water. Add the pasta to the peas and finish cooking, adding some of the reserved water if it seems too dry. Serve very hot, and serve grated parmesan separately.

It is easier to mix the pasta and peas if you break the spaghetti in 2in pieces before cooking it.

Below right: spaghetti con i piselli

Spaghetti con la balsamella · SPAGHETTI WITH BÉCHAMEL SAUCE

3 tablespoons butter
2 tablespoons flour
1¼ cups hot milk
salt and white pepper
¾ lb spaghetti
⅔ cup grated parmesan cheese

Make the *béchamel* sauce: heat 2 tablespoons (1 oz) butter and when it foams stir in the flour. Let it brown a little, then gradually stir in the hot milk. Season with salt and freshly ground white pepper and bring to a boil stirring continually. Cook over a low heat for about 15 minutes. Cook the spaghetti in plenty of boiling salted water, drain while still firm and put in a serving dish with pieces of butter and the grated cheese. Mix quickly together with the *béchamel* sauce and serve immediately.

Serves 4

Spaghetti alla carbonara · SPAGHETTI WITH BACON AND EGGS

1 cup Italian *pancetta* or bacon, cut in
  strips
¾lb spaghetti
4 egg yolks
2 tablespoons cream
grated parmesan cheese
salt and black pepper

Fry the *pancetta* strips over a moderate heat until the fat melts, then remove from the heat, drain excess fat and keep hot. Cook the spaghetti in plenty of boiling salted water. Beat the egg yolks in a bowl, add the cream, half the parmesan and plenty of freshly ground black pepper. Drain the spaghetti while still nice and firm and add to the *pancetta* in the pan. Return to the heat and mix well so the spaghetti absorbs all the flavour, then remove from the heat and quickly pour over the egg mixture, stirring so it is well blended. Serve immediately on piping hot plates and serve the remaining parmesan separately.

For a more piquant flavour use smoked bacon and *pecorino* cheese instead of parmesan.

Serves 4

Spaghetti alla carrettiera · SPAGHETTI WITH TUNA AND BACON

$\frac{1}{3}$ cup canned tuna fish, drained
$3\frac{1}{2}$ cups fresh mushrooms or
$\frac{3}{4}$ cup dried mushrooms
3 tablespoons olive oil
1 clove garlic
$\frac{1}{2}$ cup Italian *pancetta* or Canadian
  (unsmoked) bacon, cut in strips
salt and pepper
$\frac{1}{2}$ teaspoon meat extract
$\frac{3}{4}$lb spaghetti
$\frac{2}{3}$ cup grated parmesan cheese

Break up the tuna fish and slice the cleaned mushrooms (or soak dried mushrooms in warm water for about 20 minutes). Heat the olive oil and cook the garlic until brown, then add the *pancetta* strips and cook until the fat is transparent. Add the sliced mushrooms, season with salt and freshly ground pepper, then simmer for about 10 minutes with a few tablespoons of boiling water in which you have dissolved the meat extract. Add the mashed tuna fish and stir over a low heat for a few minutes. Cook the spaghetti in plenty of boiling salted water, drain while still firm and chewy then put in a hot serving dish with the sauce. Serve grated parmesan separately.

Serves 4

Above left: spaghetti alla carrettiera

Penne con i carciofi · PENNE WITH ARTICHOKES

4 tender young artichokes
juice of a lemon
4 tablespoons olive oil
1 clove garlic, finely chopped
salt and pepper
1 sprig parsley
$\frac{3}{4}$lb *penne*
1 tablespoon butter
$\frac{2}{3}$ cup grated parmesan cheese

Remove the outer leaves from the artichokes and cut off the sharp points so the tender parts remain. Cut into wedges with a sharp knife and put in a bowl of cold water with a little lemon juice. Heat the oil and 6 tablespoons water in a pan, add the finely chopped garlic, the artichoke pieces and some freshly ground pepper and simmer over a low heat, covered, until the artichokes are tender. When nearly done add the finely chopped parsley. Cook the *penne* in plenty of boiling salted water, drain while still quite firm and put in a serving dish with slathers of butter. Mix well and add the artichoke sauce. Serve grated parmesan separately.

Serves 4

Above right: penne con i carciofi

Maccheroni ai quattro formaggi · MACARONI WITH FOUR CHEESES

$\frac{1}{4}$ cup butter
$\frac{1}{2}$ teaspoon flour
$\frac{3}{4}$ cup milk
$\frac{1}{3}$ cup *mozzarella* cheese, cut in thin
  strips
$\frac{1}{3}$ cup gruyère cheese, cut in thin
  strips
$\frac{1}{3}$ cup *fontina* cheese, cut in thin
  strips
$\frac{1}{3}$ cup mild *provolone* or Dutch
  cheese, cut in thin strips
$\frac{3}{4}$lb macaroni
salt and pepper
grated parmesan cheese

Heat half the butter and when it starts to foam stir in the flour and cook for 30 seconds, then stir in the milk and simmer for about 5 minutes. Remove from the heat, beat in the cheeses and set aside. Cook the macaroni in plenty of boiling salted water, drain while still firm and put in a deep serving bowl. Sprinkle with freshly ground black pepper and dot with the remaining butter. Mix well. Reheat the cheese sauce over a good heat stirring well, then pour over the macaroni and mix rapidly. Serve very hot with grated parmesan handed round separately.

Use any other cheese according to taste, but *fontina* should always be included.

Serves 4

Below: maccheroni ai quattro formaggi

Spaghetti con capperi e olive nere · SPAGHETTI WITH CAPERS AND BLACK OLIVES

2 tablespoons capers in vinegar
2 large pitted black olives, quartered
4 tablespoons olive oil
1 hot chili pepper
1 sprig parsley
1 tablespoon tomato sauce
¾lb spaghetti

Squeeze the capers and chop well, then put in a bowl with the quartered olives and the olive oil. Remove the seeds from the chili pepper and add, in one piece, together with the chopped parsley and tomato sauce. Mix well. Cook the pasta in plenty of boiling salted water and drain while still firm and chewy. Remove the chili pepper from the sauce and serve the sauce with the pasta.

Grated cheese is not necessary with this dish.

Serves 4

Penne all'arrabbiata · PENNE WITH PIQUANT TOMATO SAUCE

1 medium onion
1 clove garlic
5 large ripe or canned (tinned) peeled
   tomatoes
¾lb *penne rigate*
salt
1 teaspoon butter
¼lb Italian *pancetta* or Canadian
   (unsmoked) bacon, cut in strips
1 hot chili pepper
½ cup grated *pecorino* cheese

Finely chop the onion and garlic. Plunge the tomatoes into boiling water and remove the skins, squeeze out the seeds and chop well or cut in thin strips. Cook the pasta in plenty of boiling salted water; put the butter in a pan with the chopped onion, garlic and *pancetta* strips and cook over a low heat until golden brown. Add the puréed tomatoes and the hot chili pepper, then simmer over a moderate heat. Remove the chili pepper when the sauce is spicy enough for your taste. Partially drain the pasta when half cooked, then add to the sauce with 1 or 2 tablespoons grated *pecorino*. Mix well and cook until the pasta is just *al dente*. If the sauce seems too dry add a few tablespoons of the pasta cooking water, then mix with the hot pasta and serve the remaining grated *pecorino* separately.

For a less piquant, but equally exquisite, flavour, use grated parmesan instead of *pecorino*.

Serves 4

Right: penne all'arrabbiata

138

Tagliatelle verdi alla marinara · TAGLIATELLE VERDI WITH MUSSELS

1¾lb mussels
4 tablespoons olive oil
¼ onion, sliced
1 clove garlic, crushed
4 ripe tomatoes
salt and pepper
chopped parsley
¾lb *tagliatelle verdi*
pinch bicarbonate of soda

Leave the mussels in a bowl under running water to clean them, then scrub well and put in a pan with one tablespoon oil. Cook over a high heat and remove as they open. Put the liquid remaining in the pan through a very fine sieve or cloth and set aside. Heat 3 tablespoons oil with the sliced onion and crushed garlic (remove the central part), then add the skinned, seeded tomatoes to the pan. Season with salt and freshly ground pepper and the chopped parsley and cook over a lively heat until the sauce is thick. Add most of the mussels and a few tablespoons of their filtered liquid.

Cook the *tagliatelle verdi* in plenty of boiling salted water and before draining add a pinch of bicarbonate of soda dissolved in a glass of cold water; this helps the pasta to stay really green and prevents it from sticking together. Mix with the sauce and serve in an attractive bowl topped with a few of the mussels and sprinkled with freshly ground black pepper.

Serves 4

Fettuccine con prosciutto e panna · FETTUCCINE WITH RAW PROSCIUTTO AND CREAM

$2\frac{3}{4}$ **cups (sifted) flour**
3 eggs
$\frac{3}{4}$ **cup heavy (double) cream**
$\frac{1}{2}$ **cup raw prosciutto, cut in thin**
  strips
$\frac{2}{3}$ **cup grated parmesan cheese**
1 egg yolk
salt and white pepper

Mix the flour, a pinch of salt and the 3 eggs and knead until smooth and firm, then roll out and cut into *fettuccine* about $\frac{1}{4}$in wide. Put the cream in a serving dish, add the prosciutto cut in strips, half the grated parmesan, the egg yolk, salt and freshly ground pepper to taste. Mix well with a wooden spoon until smooth and thick. Cook the *fettuccine* in plenty of boiling salted water, drain while firm and chewy and put in the hot serving dish. Stir gently to blend the pasta with the sauce, then serve with grated parmesan on the side.

Serves 4

Spaghetti alla boscaiola · SPAGHETTI WITH MUSHROOMS AND TOMATOES

$\frac{3}{4}$ **cup dried mushrooms**
$\frac{1}{3}$ **cup canned (tinned) tuna fish**
4 large ripe tomatoes or canned
  (tinned) peeled tomatoes
5 tablespoons olive oil
salt and pepper
2 cloves garlic
$\frac{3}{4}$**lb spaghetti**
1 sprig parsley

Soak the mushrooms in warm water for about 20 minutes. Mash the tuna fish. Plunge the tomatoes in boiling water and remove the skins, then chop, or put canned (tinned) peeled tomatoes through a food mill. Heat half the oil and add the thinly sliced mushrooms. Season with salt and freshly ground pepper and cook over moderate heat until the sauce is thick, then add the tuna fish and keep hot on one side. Meanwhile cook the pasta in plenty of boiling salted water. Put the tomato purée and finely chopped garlic in a pan with the remaining oil, season with salt and pepper and thicken over moderate heat. Mix the pasta with the tuna fish and both the sauces, add freshly chopped parsley and serve immediately. Grated cheese is not required.

Serves 4

Spaghetti alla bucaniera · SPAGHETTI WITH SEAFOOD

$\frac{1}{3}$ cup octopus or squid
$\frac{1}{3}$ cup shrimp or prawns
4 large ripe or canned (tinned) peeled
   tomatoes
2 cloves garlic
5 tablespoons olive oil
salt and pepper
$\frac{1}{4}$ cup shelled clams
$\frac{3}{4}$ lb spaghetti
1 sprig parsley

Wash and clean the octopus or squid very well and chop in small pieces. Shell and wash the shrimp or prawns. Peel the tomatoes, squeeze out the seeds and excess water and chop well, or put canned (tinned) tomatoes through a food mill. Chop the garlic in very small pieces. Heat 2 tablespoons oil with the tomatoes, garlic, salt and freshly ground pepper and simmer over a moderate heat until thick and creamy. Heat the remaining oil in another pan and fry the octopus or squid with some salt and pepper for about 10 minutes, then add the shrimp or prawns and finally the clams. Let this simmer rapidly for about 5 minutes, then remove from the heat and keep hot. Cook the spaghetti in plenty of boiling salted water, drain while still firm and mix with the sauces. Sprinkle with plenty of finely chopped parsley, mix well and serve very hot.

No grated cheese is necessary with this dish.

Serves 4

Fettuccine alla papalina · FETTUCCINE WITH RAW PROSCIUTTO AND EGGS

2¾ cups (sifted) flour
5 eggs
1 tablespoon olive oil
¾ cup lean raw prosciutto, cut in
  strips
½ onion, chopped
¼ cup butter
1 cup grated parmesan cheese
6 tablespoons cream
salt and pepper

Make a dough with the flour, 3 eggs, 1 tablespoon oil and a pinch of salt and knead well to obtain a smooth soft dough – you should hear the air bubbles pop when you cut it. Roll out to a medium thickness and cut into *fettuccine* about ⅜in wide. Cook the pasta in plenty of boiling salted water. Cut the prosciutto in fine strips and lightly brown with the chopped onion in 1 tablespoon (½oz) butter. Just before draining the pasta melt 2 tablespoons (1oz) butter in a large pan and when it starts to foam add 2 eggs beaten with 2 tablespoons grated parmesan and the cream. Stir well and add the drained pasta while the eggs are still fairly runny, then stir in the prosciutto mixture and some freshly ground pepper. Mix well and remove from the heat. Serve very hot, sprinkled with grated parmesan.

Be careful to add the pasta to the eggs and cream just at the right moment – they should not be allowed to coagulate too much.

Serves 4

Right: fettuccine alla papalina

Fettuccine alla trasteverina · FETTUCCINE WITH SEAFOOD

2¾ cups (sifted) flour
3 eggs
3 tablespoons olive oil
½ onion
1 clove garlic
1 sprig parsley
¼ cup butter
salt and pepper
4 large ripe or canned (tinned) peeled
  tomatoes
2lb small clams in their shells
⅓ cup shelled shrimp or prawns

Mix the flour, eggs, 1 teaspoon olive oil and a pinch of salt, then knead well to obtain a smooth soft dough. Roll out to a medium thickness, then roll up and cut into broad *fettuccine* about 1 in (1 finger) wide. Chop the onion, garlic, and parsley and soften in the remaining oil and half the butter. Skin, seed and chop the tomatoes, or put canned (tinned) tomatoes through a food mill. When the parsley is wilted, add to the onion. Season with salt and freshly ground pepper. Meanwhile cook the clams with a glass of water over a lively heat and remove from their shells as they open. Reserve the cooking liquid. Wash and chop the shrimp or prawns, then add to the tomatoes and cook over a moderate heat. Put the clam cooking liquid through a fine sieve or piece of gauze and add to the shrimp. Raise the heat, season with salt and pepper and reduce in volume a little. When shrimp or prawns are nearly ready add the clams. Cook the *fettuccine* in plenty of boiling salted water, drain while still firm and put in a deep serving dish with the sauce and finely chopped parsley. Mix well and serve immediately.

Serves 4

Spaghetti al gorgonzola · SPAGHETTI WITH GORGONZOLA

¾lb spaghetti, *bucatini* or *perciatelli*
2 tablespoons butter
¾ cup heavy (double) cream
¼ cup gorgonzola cheese
2 sage leaves
salt and white pepper

Cook the pasta in plenty of boiling salted water. Put the butter, cream, gorgonzola and sage in a saucepan and melt in a *bain-marie* (double boiler) so it does not boil. Stir gently and continually to obtain a smooth thick velvety cream, then remove from the heat and keep hot. Drain the pasta while still firm and chewy, put in a serving dish with the sauce (remember to remove the sage leaves) and grind over some white pepper. Mix well so the sauce is well distributed and serve very hot.

Serves 4

Above : spaghetti al gorgonzola

Spaghetti alla stallina · SPAGHETTI WITH BACON AND PECORINO CHEESE

¾lb spaghetti
1 cup Canadian (smoked) lean bacon, finely sliced
3 tablespoons olive oil
2 cloves garlic, crushed
⅔ cup grated *pecorino* cheese
salt and pepper

Cook the spaghetti in plenty of boiling salted water. Put the thin-sliced bacon in a broad pan with the oil and the crushed garlic and cook very slowly, stirring continually until the bacon fat is transparent. Drain the spaghetti while still very firm and add to the bacon to finish cooking in the fat, stirring gently. Add a little of the pasta cooking water if the mixture seems too dry. When nearly done add the grated *pecorino* and a little freshly ground pepper. Mix well and serve very hot.

Serves 4

Spaghetti tutto mare · SPAGHETTI WITH SEAFOOD

2 large ripe or canned (tinned) peeled tomatoes
½ cup mushrooms, sliced
1 small onion
1 small carrot
1 sprig parsley
5 tablespoons olive oil
¾lb seafood (baby squid, clams, shrimp or prawns and cooked shelled mussels)
6 tablespoons dry white wine
1 small piece hot chili
salt and pepper
¾lb spaghetti

Peel the tomatoes, squeeze out the seeds and chop the tomatoes coarsely, or put canned (tinned) tomatoes through a food mill. Clean and slice the mushrooms. Chop the onion, carrot and a little parsley. Heat 2 tablespoons oil and lightly brown the chopped squid, then add half the wine and let it evaporate over a good heat. Add the tomatoes, hot chili pepper and a pinch of salt and cook until the squid are tender. When nearly done remove the hot pepper and add the mushrooms. Meanwhile heat the remaining oil and soften the chopped vegetables, then add the clams, shrimp or prawns and mussels, and some salt to taste. Pour over the remaining wine, let it evaporate and cook for a few more minutes.

Cook the spaghetti in plenty of boiling salted water, drain while still nice and firm and put in a serving bowl with the seafood sauce. Sprinkle with plenty of finely chopped parsley and mix well.

No cheese is served with this dish.

Serves 4

Below : spaghetti tutto mare

146

Lasagnette al mascarpone · LASAGNETTE WITH MASCARPONE CHEESE

2¾ cups (sifted) flour
3 eggs
2 egg yolks
3 tablespoons olive oil
½ cup very fresh *mascarpone* (semi-soft cheese)
salt and pepper
⅔ cup grated parmesan cheese

Mix the flour and eggs and a pinch of salt to obtain a smooth, firm dough and roll out to a medium thickness. Roll up and cut into *lasagnette* about 1 in wide. Leave to dry on a floured pastry board or cloth. Cook in plenty of boiling salted water. Beat the egg yolks and gradually add the olive oil drop by drop, as for mayonnaise, then beating more slowly gradually add the *mascarpone* with a pinch of salt and some freshly ground black pepper. Drain the *lasagnette* while nice and firm, then put in a serving bowl with the sauce and mix well. Sprinkle with grated parmesan and serve immediately.

Serves 4

Above: lasagnette al mascarpone

Maccheroni alla erbe aromatiche · MACARONI WITH HERBS

½ cup raw prosciutto fat, chopped
1 lb lean veal
1 clove garlic
1 medium onion
1 small carrot
2 medium stalks celery
1 sprig parsley
2 or 3 basil leaves
2 tablespoons butter
3 tablespoons olive oil
6 tablespoons dry white wine
1 teaspoon meat extract
2 tablespoons concentrated tomato paste (purée)
salt and pepper
1 piece hot chili pepper
¾ lb macaroni
⅔ cup grated parmesan cheese

Cut the prosciutto fat into thin slices and wrap around the veal. Finely chop the garlic, onion, carrot, celery, parsley and basil. Heat the butter and oil in an earthenware or other casserole and brown the veal on all sides over a moderate heat. Moisten with wine, raise the heat and let it evaporate uncovered. Add the chopped vegetables and cook a little, stirring occasionally. Pour in some water with the meat extract and the tomato paste (purée). Season with salt and freshly ground pepper, add the hot chili pepper (cut lengthwise with the seeds removed), and simmer gently covered until the sauce is smooth and thick.

Cook the macaroni in plenty of boiling salted water, drain while still firm and put in a serving dish with some of the meat, cut into pieces, and some grated parmesan. Slice the rest of the meat and cover with the remaining sauce to make a second course; serve with a green salad.

Serves 4

Below: maccheroni alle erbe aromatiche

Insalata di penne · PENNE IN SALAD

¾lb smooth *penne*
2 hard-boiled eggs
1 large firm tomato
1 small can (tin) of tuna fish, about
   ¼lb
12 black olives
8 stuffed olives
1 sweet pepper in vinegar
4 tablespoons olive oil

This is a delicious summer dish.

Cook the pasta in plenty of boiling salted water. Meanwhile prepare the other ingredients: cut the eggs and tomatoes in quarters, mash the tuna fish with a fork, pit (stone) the black olives, cut the stuffed olives in half and dice the sweet pepper. Drain the pasta and put in a serving bowl with the olive oil and all the other ingredients except the eggs and tomatoes. Mix well and decorate with the tomato and egg quarters. No grated cheese is necessary.

Serves 4

Right : insalata di penne

Tagliatelle col pollo · TAGLIATELLE WITH CHICKEN

2¾ cups (sifted) flour
3 eggs
1 young chicken, about 3lb
4 tablespoons olive oil
¼ cup butter
1 small onion
6 tablespoons dry red wine
¾ cup milk
1 teaspoon meat extract
salt and pepper
1 tablespoon concentrated tomato
   paste (purée)
⅔ cup grated parmesan cheese

Mix the flour, eggs and a pinch of salt and knead to make a smooth elastic dough — you should hear the air bubbles pop when you cut it. Roll out not too thinly and leave to dry a little, then roll up and cut in strips about 1 in wide. Clean and bone the chicken and cut in serving pieces. Heat the oil and butter and brown the chopped onion, then brown the chicken pieces on all sides. Raise the heat, add the wine and let it evaporate, then pour in the milk in which you have dissolved the meat extract. Season with salt and freshly ground black pepper, then simmer for about 15 minutes. Dilute the concentrated tomato paste (purée) with a little warm water and add to the sauce; cook slowly, adding more warm water if it seems too dry, until the chicken is tender. The sauce should be smooth and not too thick.

Cook the *tagliatelle* in plenty of boiling salted water, drain while still firm and chewy and put in a hot serving dish with the sauce and sprinkle with parmesan. Serve the chicken pieces as a second course with new potatoes and a green salad.

Serves 4

Spaghettini rapidi di mezzanotte · QUICK MIDNIGHT SPAGHETTINI

6 large ripe or canned (tinned) peeled tomatoes
salt
1 hot chili pepper
¾ lb *spaghettini*
4 tablespoons olive oil
⅔ cup grated parmesan cheese

Plunge the tomatoes in boiling water to remove the skins, cut in half and squeeze out the seeds and juice, then break with your hands and put in a pan with a little salt and the chili pepper, sliced lengthwise to remove the seeds. (If using canned (tinned) tomatoes, put through a food mill.) Simmer gently to obtain a thick sauce. Cook the *spaghettini* in plenty of boiling salted water, drain well and put in a deep serving bowl with the olive oil. Remove the chili pepper and mix the tomato sauce with the pasta. Serve with grated parmesan.

This is an ideal midnight dish as the sauce is light and easy to prepare and has a deliciously refreshing flavour. If you use tinned peeled tomatoes the sauce will cook in the same time as the *spaghettini*.

Serves 4

Soufflé di spaghetti · SPAGHETTI SOUFFLÉ

¾ lb spaghetti
¼ cup butter
4 tablespoons flour
¾ cup warm milk
salt and pepper
⅔ cup grated parmesan cheese
4 egg whites
2 egg yolks

Cook the spaghetti in plenty of boiling salted water. Heat the butter (reserving 1 tablespoon (½oz)); when it starts to foam stir in the flour so it doesn't make any lumps and when golden brown slowly add the warm milk, stirring constantly. Season with salt and freshly ground pepper. Mix well and simmer for about 5 minutes until smooth and thick. Remove from the heat and leave to cool, then add the grated parmesan and stir in the 2 egg yolks, one at a time, and mix well. Drain the spaghetti while still firm and chewy and mix with the egg and cheese mixture, then leave to cool. Beat the 4 egg whites until stiff and fold into the spaghetti mixture. Pour gently into a soufflé dish, which you have greased with the remaining butter, then bake in a moderate oven for about 30 minutes; do not open the oven door while it is cooking.

Serves 4

Gnocchi con ragù di carne · GNOCCHI WITH MEAT SAUCE

6 medium potatoes
2   cups (sifted) flour
2 eggs
1 teaspoon salt
$\frac{1}{4}$ cup butter
$\frac{1}{2}$ onion
1 small piece of celery
1 sprig parsley
$\frac{1}{2}$lb lean ground (minced) beef
4 large ripe or canned (tinned) peeled
   tomatoes
salt and pepper
1 cup grated parmesan cheese

Cook the potatoes, peel while still hot and put through a food mill or potato ricer so they fall on to a pastry board or working surface. Mix in the flour, eggs and 1 teaspoon salt, kneading well to make a smooth, elastic dough which does not stick to your hands. Roll out and cut into $1\frac{1}{4}$in pieces. Sprinkle with flour and press deftly with your thumb against the back of a fork so they drop on to the board.

Make a simple, tasty meat sauce: heat the butter and brown the very fine, chopped vegetables for a few minutes, then add the ground (minced) beef and cook for 5 minutes stirring continually. Add the puréed tomatoes, season with salt and freshly ground pepper and cook until thick over a low heat. Cook the *gnocchi* in plenty of boiling salted water for about 8–10 minutes, drain and serve in a deep bowl with the meat sauce. Serve grated parmesan separately.

Serves 4

Spaghetti alla contadina · SPAGHETTI WITH SALAMI AND GREEN BEANS

2 carrots, diced
1¾ cups green beans, diced (chopped)
1 medium onion
1 stalk celery
¼ cup butter
salt and pepper
6 tablespoons dry white wine
4 ripe tomatoes
2 thick slices salami, diced
¾ lb spaghetti
⅔ cup grated parmesan cheese

Cook the diced carrots and beans in lightly salted boiling water and drain while still quite firm. Dice (finely chop) the onion and celery and brown in the butter, then add the carrots and beans. Season with salt and freshly ground pepper, then cook for a few minutes. Raise the heat, add the wine and let it evaporate. Add the tomatoes, breaking after peeling, in large pieces, squeezing out the seeds. Season with salt and simmer until the sauce is thick, adding the diced salami just before you remove the pan from the heat.

Cook the spaghetti in plenty of boiling salted water, drain while still firm and put in a deep serving dish with the sauce and half the grated parmesan. Mix well and serve with the remaining grated cheese.

Serves 4

Maccheroni alla napoletana · MACARONI WITH MOZZARELLA AND TOMATO SAUCE

1 clove garlic
1 medium onion
5 large ripe or canned (tinned) peeled
  tomatoes
$\frac{1}{3}$ cup butter
salt and pepper
$\frac{3}{4}$lb macaroni
1$\frac{1}{4}$ cups fresh *scamorza* cheese or
  mozzarella cheese, sliced

Finely chop the garlic and onion. Put the tomatoes through a food mill and put in a pan with the garlic, onion and $\frac{1}{4}$ cup (2 oz) butter. Season with salt and freshly ground pepper and cook over a moderate heat until thick. Half-cook the macaroni in plenty of boiling salted water, then drain well. Put alternate layers of macaroni, sliced *scamorza* or *mozzarella* and tomato sauce in a greased ovenproof dish, ending with a layer of tomato sauce. Dot with remaining butter and bake in a hot oven (about 400°F) for about 40 minutes. Serve very hot.

Serves 4

Penne vesuviane · PENNE WITH TOMATO SAUCE

¾lb *penne rigate*
4 large ripe or canned (tinned) peeled
   tomatoes
12 black olives
1 *mozzarella* cheese
1 clove garlic
1 sprig basil
salt and pepper
4 tablespoons olive oil
2 tablespoons capers, drained
1 pinch oregano

Cook the *penne* in plenty of boiling, salted water. Put the tomatoes through a food mill; pit (stone) the olives and cut in half. Dice (chop) the *mozzarella* and crush the clove of garlic. Put the puréed tomatoes in a pan with the garlic and a few leaves of basil and season with a little salt. Cook over a good heat until thick, then remove the garlic and remove from the heat. Drain the *penne* while still firm and put in a deep serving bowl with the oil and a little freshly ground pepper. Mix quickly, then stir in the capers, olives and *mozzarella*. Pour over the hot tomato sauce, sprinkle wih oregano and serve immediately. Decorate with a few basil leaves to add a nice colour contrast.

No grated cheese is served with this dish.

Serves 4

Above : penne vesuviane

Vermicelli alla francese · VERMICELLI WITH HAM AND PEAS

1 onion
½ **cup cooked ham, finely chopped**
¼ **cup butter**
1¼ cups fresh (shelled) or canned
   (tinned) peas
salt and pepper
sugar
1 bouillon cube
½ **teaspoon meat extract**
6 tablespoons red wine
¾lb *vermicelli*
⅔ **cup grated parmesan cheese**

Slice the onion and dice the ham so that you have the fat and lean together. Heat the butter and brown the ham and onion over a low heat until the onion is soft and transparent. Add the peas, season with a little salt, pepper and sugar and stir in the bouillon cube or meat extract dissolved in a little water. Cook over a lively heat until the peas are almost done, then add the wine and diced ham. Let the wine evaporate and remove from the heat. Cook the *vermicelli* and drain while nice and firm, then mix with the peas and serve with plenty of grated parmesan. If you use canned (tinned) peas they need only cook 3 or 4 minutes before you add the wine and diced ham.

Serves 4

Below : vermicelli alla francese

Spaghetti con olive · SPAGHETTI WITH OLIVES

1 cup bacon, cut in strips
¾ lb spaghetti
1 clove garlic
1 stalk celery
1 teaspoon meat extract
salt and pepper
1½ cups green olives
2 tablespoons olive oil
⅔ cup grated parmesan cheese

Cut the bacon in thin strips and chop the garlic and the celery into small pieces. While the spaghetti is cooking in plenty of boiling salted water heat the bacon in a frying pan with the garlic and celery for 3 or 4 minutes, then add ¾ cup (6 fl oz) warm water in which you have dissolved the meat extract. Season with salt and freshly ground pepper and simmer covered for about 10 minutes. Pit (stone) the olives and chop most of them, reserving some whole. Drain the spaghetti while still firm and chewy, put in a serving dish with the oil and bacon and the chopped and whole olives. Serve grated parmesan on the side.

Serves 4

Lasagnette agli spinaci · LASAGNETTE WITH SPINACH

1lb uncooked spinach
$\frac{1}{4}$ cup butter
2 tablespoons olive oil
1 clove garlic, crushed
salt and pepper
$1\frac{1}{3}$ cups grated parmesan cheese
$\frac{1}{2}$lb *lasagnette* (see recipe p.149)

Wash the spinach very well and cook for a few minutes in very little water with a little salt to keep it nice and green. Drain well and chop. Heat the butter and oil and brown the crushed garlic, then remove garlic from the pan. Add the spinach, season with salt and freshly ground pepper and cook for a few minutes, then stir in half the grated parmesan. Cook the *lasagnette* in plenty of boiling salted water and drain while still firm. Put the pasta into a serving dish and cover evenly with the spinach. Serve the remaining grated parmesan separately.

Serves 4

Penne al mascarpone · PENNE WITH MASCARPONE CHEESE

$\frac{3}{4}$lb *penne rigate*
2 tablespoons butter
salt
$\frac{2}{3}$ cup grated parmesan cheese
$\frac{1}{3}$ cup fresh *mascarpone* (semi-soft cheese)
$\frac{1}{2}$ cup lean cooked ham, finely chopped

Cook the *penne* in plenty of boiling salted water until tender but still firm, then remove the pan from the heat and pour in $\frac{1}{2}$ pint cold water to stop the pasta sticking together. Drain and put in a deep serving dish. Melt the butter and mix with the *penne* together with the grated parmesan. Dot with pieces of *mascarpone*, sprinkle the finely chopped ham overall and serve immediately.

Serves 4

Right: penne al mascarpone

Paglia e fieno (Straw and Hay) · WHITE AND GREEN PASTA

2 cups spinach
$3\frac{1}{4}$ cups (sifted) flour
3 eggs
2 tablespoons butter
$\frac{1}{2}$ cup cooked ham, finely chopped
$\frac{3}{4}$ cup heavy (double) cream
salt

Wash the spinach very well and discard the stalks, then cook in a little lightly salted water. Drain, squeeze out the moisture and put through a food mill. Make a firm dough with the flour, eggs and a pinch of salt, then knead until smooth and elastic and divide into 2 unequal parts and leave the smaller part to dry a little. Roll out the large amount not too thinly, leave to dry a little, then cut into *fettuccine* about $\frac{1}{2}$in wide. Knead the remaining dough with the spinach purée, adding a little extra flour, then roll out and cut into *tagliatelle* the same size as the white pasta. Cook in plenty of boiling salted water.

Melt the butter and lightly brown the diced ham until the fat is transparent, then stir in the cream. Season with salt, simmer for 2 minutes and meanwhile drain the pasta. Put the pasta in the pan with the ham and stir gently until the pasta is a perfect consistency. Serve sprinkled with plenty of grated parmesan.

Serves 4

STUFFED PASTA RECIPES

Ravioli con la zucca · RAVIOLI WITH PUMPKIN

2lb pumpkin
½lb calf's brains
½ cup raw prosciutto, chopped
5 tablespoons butter
¾ cup lean veal
salt and pepper
5 eggs
½ cup very fresh *ricotta* cheese
2¾ cups (sifted) flour
⅔ cup grated parmesan cheese

Cook the pumpkin in boiling salted water, drain very well and cut off the hard green part, then chop the soft flesh into very small pieces. Blanch the brains for 5 minutes, remove the outer membrane and chop well. Chop the raw prosciutto. Heat 2 tablespoons butter (1oz) and brown the veal; season with salt and freshly ground pepper and cook until the veal is tender, adding a few tablespoons of water if it seems too dry. Let cool and put through food mill. Beat 2 of the eggs well in a bowl and stir in the brains and ground (minced) veal with the juice from the pan, together with the crumbled *ricotta* and chopped ham and pumpkin. Season with salt to taste and stir well with a wooden spoon to make a smooth, fairly firm filling. Mix the flour, the 3 remaining eggs and a pinch of salt on a pastry board and knead well to obtain a smooth elastic dough. Roll out fairly thinly and put small spoonfulls of the filling at regular intervals on half the dough. Brush the spaces in between with water then fold over the other half of the dough and press down between the mounds of filling so the two sheets stick together. Cut into squares of ravioli with a pasta wheel. Cook in plenty of boiling salted water and remove with a slotted spoon when they are cooked. Pour melted butter over each helping and serve with grated parmesan.

Serves 4

Ravioli agli ortaggi · RAVIOLI WITH VEGETABLES

½lb zucchini (courgettes)
2 sticks celery
1¾ **cups green beans, finely chopped**
1 cup bacon, cut in strips
1 cup fresh or canned (tinned) green beans
1¼ **cups shelled peas**
½ **teaspoon meat extract**
salt and pepper
¾**lb ravioli (see basic recipe, p. 44)**
⅔ **cup grated parmesan cheese**

Wash and pick over the vegetables; slice the zucchini (courgettes) not too thinly, dice (chop) the celery and beans into 1in pieces. Fry the bacon until the fat is transparent over a low heat, then remove from the pan with a fork and keep hot. Cook the vegetables in the bacon fat, stirring occasionally for a few minutes, then pour over the meat extract dissolved in 3 tablespoons water. Season with salt and freshly ground pepper and cook over a good heat, stirring continually, until the liquid is reduced and the vegetables are tender but not mushy. When nearly done return the bacon to the pan. Cook the ravioli in plenty of boiling salted water, drain and put in a deep serving dish with the vegetables and all the sauce. Serve grated parmesan separately.

Serves 4

Ravioli di magro alla panna · LENTEN RAVIOLI WITH CREAM

2 cups spinach
$\frac{1}{4}$ cup butter
salt and pepper
$\frac{1}{2}$ cup very fresh *ricotta* cheese
2$\frac{3}{4}$ cups (sifted) flour
3 eggs
$\frac{3}{4}$ cup cream
$\frac{2}{3}$ cup grated parmesan cheese

Wash the spinach well and remove the stalks, then cook in very little lightly salted water. Drain, squeeze out liquid then chop well. Heat 1 tablespoon ($\frac{1}{2}$oz) butter and add the spinach. Season with salt and pepper and cook for about 4 minutes. Put the *ricotta* in a bowl with the spinach and work together with a wooden spoon to make a smooth, creamy mixture. Check the seasoning, adding more salt to taste, then set aside. Make the ravioli as in the basic recipe on page 44 with the flour, eggs and a pinch of salt, and stuff with the spinach filling. Cook in plenty of boiling salted water and drain while still firm and chewy. Heat the remainder of the butter and the cream until they boil, then pour in the hot ravioli, stirring with two wooden forks so the pasta absorbs all the flavour. Stir in half the grated parmesan and serve immediately; hand round the remaining parmesan separately.

Serves 4

Above: ravioli di magro alla panna

Ravioli all'abruzzese · RAVIOLI WITH RICOTTA AND MEAT SAUCE

5 eggs
2 teaspoons sugar
pinch cinnamon
1$\frac{1}{2}$ cups *ricotta* cheese
3$\frac{1}{4}$ cups (sifted) flour
$\frac{1}{4}$ cup butter
$\frac{1}{2}$ cup ground (minced) beef or veal
1 onion, chopped
1 clove garlic, finely chopped
1 clove
salt and pepper
4 tablespoons dry white wine
4 tablespoons concentrated tomato paste (purée)
$\frac{1}{2}$ teaspoon meat extract
$\frac{2}{3}$ cup grated parmesan cheese

Beat one of the eggs with the sugar and stir in a pinch of cinnamon and the *ricotta* to make a soft filling for the ravioli.

Mix the flour and 3 eggs; knead very well to obtain a smooth elastic dough, then roll out thin. Beat the remaining egg with some water and brush on the half of the dough where you will put the mounds of fillings. Put little spoonfuls of filling at regular intervals on the dough and fold over the other half, pressing down firmly in between the mounds, then cut into squares. Leave to dry on the floured table.

Heat the butter until it browns, then add the ground (minced) meat, chopped onion and very finely chopped garlic and the clove. Season with salt and freshly ground pepper and brown the meat all over, stirring continually. Add the wine; let it evaporate over a good heat, then remove the clove and add the concentrated tomato paste (purée) and the meat extract diluted in a little warm water. Cook, covered, over a low heat until the sauce is nice and thick. Cook the ravioli in plenty of boiling salted water and remove with a slotted spoon when they are done. Pour some hot sauce on each helping and serve grated parmesan separately.

For a more piquant flavour use grated *pecorino* cheese instead of parmesan.

Serves 4

Below: ravioli all'abruzzese

Maccheroni ripieni · STUFFED MACARONI

1 onion
1 sprig parsley
$\frac{1}{4}$lb sweetbreads
$\frac{1}{4}$ cup butter
1 chicken breast
$\frac{1}{4}$lb lean veal
salt and pepper
3 tablespoons bread crumbs
3 tablespoons milk
4 tablespoons grated parmesan
4 eggs
2$\frac{1}{4}$ cups (sifted) flour
$\frac{3}{4}$–1 cup stock

Chop the onion and parsley. Blanch the sweetbreads for about 5 minutes in boiling salted water, then remove the outer membrane and chop coarsely. Heat 2 tablespoons (1oz) butter and brown the chicken breast and veal on all sides, stirring occasionally. Add the chopped onion and parsley, 2 tablespoons water and some salt and pepper and simmer gently, stirring frequently for about 20 minutes. If it seems too dry add a little more water. Soak the bread crumbs in the milk, then add 2 tablespoons grated parmesan. When the meat is cooked, bone, chop and put through a food mill with the onion and parsley, then mix in the bread and parmesan, together with the chopped sweetbreads. Stir in 2 egg yolks and 1 egg white to bind, season with salt and mix until you have a smooth, firm filling.

Put the flour in a mound on a pastry board or working surface with a pinch of salt and the 2 remaining eggs and 1 egg white, then knead very well to obtain a smooth elastic dough. Roll out to a medium thickness and cut into 2$\frac{1}{2}$–3in squares. Put a little of the filling on each square and roll up gently to make a small pancake. Press the edges together, moisten with a little milk or water if the pasta seems too dry and arrange in a greased ovenproof dish so they are not too tightly packed, then pour the boiling stock over all. Bake in a medium oven for about 30 minutes until most of the liquid has been absorbed. Dot with the remaining butter, and sprinkle with parmesan, then return to the oven and cook until the pasta is done and the top is golden brown.

This dish can also be made with commercial *cannelloni*. Follow the instructions on the packet as to whether to boil them first or just cook them in the stock.

Serves 4

Above: maccheroni ripieni

Vol-au-vent con tortellini alla panna · VOL-AU-VENT WITH TORTELLINI AND CREAM

4 large individual *vol-au-vent* cases
$\frac{3}{4}$lb commercial *tortellini*
salt
2 tablespoons butter
$\frac{3}{4}$ cup cream
$\frac{2}{3}$ cup grated parmesan cheese

Use ready-made medium-sized *vol-au-vent* cases or make them yourself with frozen puff pastry. The *tortellini* can be home-made as in *agnolotti toscani* (page 172), or bought. Cook them in plenty of boiling salted water and drain well. Heat the butter and cream and add the *tortellini*, stirring well so they absorb all the flavour. Salt to taste. Heat the *vol-au-vent* cases thoroughly, fill with the hot *tortellini*, top with parmesan and return to the oven for about 3 minutes.

This is a delicious and attractive dish.

Serves 4

Below: vol-au-vent con tortellini alla panna

Raviolini alla milanese · RAVIOLINI WITH MEAT FILLING

$\frac{1}{2}$ cup butter
$\frac{3}{4}$lb lean beef (round or chuck)
1 sprig rosemary
salt and pepper
1 thin slice raw prosciutto
4 eggs
$\frac{2}{3}$ cup grated parmesan cheese
1 pinch cinnamon
2$\frac{3}{4}$ cups (sifted) flour

Heat 3 tablespoons (1$\frac{1}{2}$ oz) butter and brown the beef with the rosemary over a good heat, then season with salt and pepper and cook, covered, over a low heat until the meat is tender, adding a little water if it seems too dry.

Finely chop the prosciutto and the cooked beef, then mix in a bowl together with 1 egg, 1 tablespoon grated parmesan, a little of the sauce from the pan where the beef has been cooking and a pinch of cinnamon to taste. Mix well and use to stuff the *raviolini*, made as on page 44 with the flour, 3 eggs and a pinch of salt. Melt the remaining butter with the beef gravy and keep hot. Cook the *raviolini* in plenty of boiling salted water, drain while still firm and put some meat sauce and plenty of grated parmesan on each helping.

Serves 4

Pansoti con la salsa di noci alla ligure · PANSOTI WITH WALNUTS

1 lb Swiss chard and borage
1 clove garlic
1 egg
$\frac{1}{2}$ cup very fresh *ricotta* cheese
$\frac{2}{3}$ cup grated parmesan cheese
salt and pepper
$2\frac{3}{4}$ cups (sifted) flour
6 tablespoons dry white wine
$1\frac{1}{4}$ cups walnuts
2 tablespoons bread crumbs
4 tablespoons olive oil
4 tablespoons soured milk

Wash the chard and borage very well, remove the stalks and cook in very little salted water, then squeeze well and put through a food mill. Chop the garlic and put in a bowl with the chard, borage, egg, ricotta and $\frac{1}{3}$ cup (1oz) grated parmesan. Season with salt and freshly ground pepper and mix until well blended.

Make the pasta dough with the flour, wine, a pinch of salt and some water, and knead until smooth and firm. Roll out not too thin and cut into 3in triangles. Put a little of the filling on each triangle, fold in two and press the edges well together to make *pansoti*.

Blanch the walnuts for a few minutes to remove the outer skin, then pound in a mortar with the bread crumbs previously soaked in water and squeezed dry, and a little salt, to obtain a smooth thick sauce. Stir in the olive oil and curdled milk (if used). Cook the *pansoti* in plenty of boiling salted water, drain well and mix with the walnut sauce in a heated serving dish. Serve hot with the remainder of the grated parmesan.

Serves 4

Casonsèi bergamaschi · CASONSÈI WITH SPINACH AND SAUSAGE FILLING

10oz uncooked spinach
$\frac{1}{4}$ cup butter
$\frac{1}{2}$ onion
1 tablespoon chopped parsley
1 clove garlic
2–3 medium potatoes
2 tablespoons dry breadcrumbs
1$\frac{1}{3}$ cups grated parmesan cheese
4 eggs
$\frac{1}{2}$ cup fresh pork sausage meat,
  cooked
salt and pepper
2$\frac{3}{4}$ cups (sifted) flour

Make the filling 24 hours in advance. Wash the spinach and cook in very little water; drain and chop well, then cook in 1 tablespoon ($\frac{1}{2}$oz) butter together with the chopped onion, chopped parsley and garlic. Boil the potatoes, peel and put through a potato ricer or food mill, then mix with the breadcrumbs, $\frac{2}{3}$ cup (2oz) grated parmesan, the spinach, 1 egg, and the finely crumbled cooked sausage meat. Season with salt and pepper and mix well, then leave covered in a cool place for 24 hours.

Make the pasta dough in the usual way with the flour, 3 eggs and a pinch of salt. Knead very well until smooth and elastic and roll out fairly thin. Use a special pasta cutter or the rim of a thin glass to cut into circles and put about $\frac{1}{2}$ tablespoon filling on each circle, then fold one edge inside, cover with the other edge and so on to make little parcels. Cook in plenty of boiling salted water for about 5 minutes, then drain and serve sprinkled with the remaining grated parmesan and the remaining butter, melted.

Any leftovers of the pasta dough can be made into *maltagliati* and served on their own or in *consommé*.

Serves 4

Anolini alla parmigiana · ANOLINI WITH BEEF FILLING

1 small carrot
1 stick celery
1 clove garlic
1 medium onion
½ cup butter
1 tablespoon olive oil
¾lb lean beef
6 tablespoons dry red wine
salt and pepper
1 tablespoon concentrated tomato
   paste (purée)
5 tablespoons dry breadcrumbs
⅔ cup grated parmesan cheese
4 eggs
grated nutmeg and cinnamon
2¾ cups (sifted) flour

Finely chop the carrot, celery, garlic and onion, then cook gently in 3 tablespoons (1½oz) butter and the oil. Add the meat and brown on all sides over a good heat. Moisten with the wine and let it evaporate, then lower the heat, season with salt and freshly ground pepper and add the concentrated tomato paste (purée) diluted in a little hot water. Simmer covered until the meat is tender and the sauce is strong and thick. Put the breadcrumbs and ½ cup (1½oz) grated parmesan in a bowl and stir in the meat sauce (*not* the meat), and 1 whole egg, to make a firm filling. Add a little nutmeg and cinnamon to taste.

Make the pasta dough with the flour, eggs and a pinch of salt. Roll out and cut into small circles, then put ½ tablespoon filling on each circle. Fold in two and press the edges well together so none of the filling escapes while they are cooking. Cook the *anolini* in plenty of boiling salted water, drain when perfectly *al dente* and put on individual plates with a few tablespoons of meat sauce and plenty of grated parmesan on each helping. Cut the meat in thin slices and serve as a second course with new potatoes or green salad

Serves 4

Timballo di tortellini · TORTELLINI PIE

1 small onion
1 sprig parsley
1 stick celery
1 small carrot
½ cup butter
¼ lb ground (minced) lean veal
6 tablespoons white wine
1¾ cups canned (tinned) peeled
    tomatoes
salt and pepper
¼ cup chicken livers
½ cup raw prosciutto, chopped finely
1¼ cups (sifted) flour
¼ cup sugar
¾ lb fresh *tortellini*, made as in
    cappelletti all'uso di Romagna,
    page 173
⅔ cup grated parmesan cheese

Chop the onion, parsley, celery and carrot. Heat 2 tablespoons (1oz) butter until it browns, then add the chopped vegetables and veal. Brown throughout then add the wine and let it evaporate over a good heat. Lower the heat and add the tomatoes, which have been put through a food mill; season with salt and freshly ground pepper and simmer covered to obtain a thick meat sauce, stirring occasionally so it does not burn. When nearly done add the chopped chicken livers and diced prosciutto and cook for a further 5 minutes.

Make a smooth dough with the flour, ⅓ cup (3oz) melted butter, the sugar and a pinch of salt. Leave covered for about 30 minutes then roll out into two sheets of pastry, one the same size as your pie pan (pie dish) and the other slightly smaller to make the pie lid. Cook the *tortellini* in plenty of boiling salted water, drain and keep on one side. Grease the pie pan (pie dish), sprinkle with flour and line with the large sheet of pastry so it comes right up to the top of the pan (dish). Fill with layers of *tortellini* and some meat sauce and grated parmesan. Dot the top layer with butter, cover with the pastry lid, pressing the edges well together, and bake in a moderate oven for about 20 minutes.

Serves 4

Agnolotti toscani · AGNOLOTTI WITH VEAL FILLING

1½ slices stale bread without the crust
a few tablespoons warm milk
¼ lb calf's brains
⅓ cup butter
½ cup ground (minced) lean veal
salt and pepper
5 level tablespoons grated parmesan
    cheese
2¾ cups (sifted) flour
4 eggs

Soak the stale bread in the warm milk. Blanch the brains in boiling water for a few minutes to remove the outer membrane. Heat 2 tablespoons (1oz) butter and cook the veal, covered, with some salt, pepper and a little water. Squeeze out the bread slightly and mix with 1 beaten egg, the chopped brain, ground (minced) cooked veal and 2 tablespoons grated parmesan. Season with salt and a little pepper if necessary and stir well to make a smooth filling. Make the *agnolotti* as in the basic recipe on page 44 and stuff with this filling. Cook in plenty of boiling salted water, drain and put in a serving bowl with the remaining melted butter and the rest of the grated parmesan.

These *agnolotti* are also very good cooked in a strong beef stock.

Serves 4

Cappelletti all'uso di Romagna · CAPPELLETTI WITH CHICKEN AND RICOTTA FILLING

2 chicken breasts
½ cup butter
salt and pepper
½ cup fresh *ricotta* cheese
1 pinch nutmeg
4 eggs
2¾ cups (sifted) flour
⅔ cup grated parmesan cheese

Brown the chicken breasts in 3 tablespoons (1½oz) butter, season with salt and freshly ground pepper and cook with a few tablespoons hot water. When the chicken is tender chop very well and mix in a bowl with the ricotta, nutmeg, 1 egg and salt to taste.

Mix the flour, 3 eggs and a pinch of salt and knead to make a soft, elastic dough, then roll out fairly thin and cut into rounds with a pasta cutter or the rim of a thin glass. Put a little filling on each circle, double over, press the edges together using a little water to seal them, then draw the 2 ends together to make little crescents or *cappelletti* (hats). Cook in plenty of boiling salted water and drain while nice and firm, then serve with the rest of the butter, melted, and grated parmesan or a good meat sauce.

Serves 4

Culingiones sardi (ravioli) · RAVIOLI WITH PECORINO AND SPINACH FILLING

4 cups spinach, chopped
$\frac{1}{4}$ cup butter
pinch nutmeg
salt and pepper
1$\frac{1}{4}$ cups soft fresh *pecorino sardo*
1 tablespoon flour
2 cups finely ground durum wheat flour
5 eggs
5 large or ripe or canned (tinned) peeled tomatoes
$\frac{1}{2}$ cup grated hard *pecorino* cheese

Wash the spinach and cook with a little water, then squeeze out, chop well and cook with 1 tablespoon ($\frac{1}{2}$oz) butter, a pinch of nutmeg, some freshly ground pepper and a little salt. Put in a bowl with 2 eggs the crumbled fresh *pecorino* and 1 tablespoon flour to bind. Work well together with a wooden spoon until smooth and firm.

Make the ravioli with the durum wheat flour, 3 eggs and a pinch of salt as in the basic recipe on page 44 and stuff with this filling. Cook in plenty of boiling salted water, put in a deep serving bowl with the remaining butter mixed with the puréed tomatoes and cooked with a pinch of salt over a moderate heat. Serve grated hard *pecorino* separately.

For a less piquant flavour use parmesan instead of *pecorino* and mix with just melted butter instead of tomato sauce.

Serves 4

Right: culingiones sardi

Gnocchi di Romagna (detti "ravioli") · GNOCCHI OR "RAVIOLI" ROMAGNA STYLE

$\frac{1}{2}$ cup very fresh *ricotta* cheese
2 eggs
1 cup grated parmesan cheese
$\frac{1}{2}$ cup (sifted) flour
salt
$\frac{1}{4}$ cup butter

These traditional "ravioli" from Romagna are not in fact made with the usual pasta dough and filling.

Mix the *ricotta*, eggs, $\frac{1}{4}$ cup (1$\frac{1}{2}$oz) grated parmesan and the flour with a little salt to taste. Work together very well with a wooden spoon then put on a floured board and make into little rolls about $\frac{1}{2}$in long. Cut these into $\frac{1}{4}$in slices and leave on a floured board so they do not stick together. Cook in plenty of boiling unsalted water, remove with a slotted spoon as they rise to the surface and be careful they do not break, then put in a dish with the melted butter and grated parmesan.

Serves 4

Agnolotti alla marchigiana · AGNOLOTTI WITH BEEF, SPINACH AND MORTADELLA FILLING

2$\frac{3}{4}$ cups (sifted) flour
3 eggs
$\frac{1}{2}$ cup butter
$\frac{1}{2}$lb ground (minced) lean beef
$\frac{3}{4}$lb spinach
1 slice *mortadella*
salt and pepper
5 large ripe or canned (tinned) peeled tomatoes
$\frac{2}{3}$ cup grated parmesan cheese

Make the *agnolotti* as in the basic recipe on page 44, with the following filling. Heat 1 tablespoon ($\frac{1}{2}$oz) butter and brown the ground (minced) beef with a pinch of salt, then transfer to a mixing bowl. Wash the spinach and discard the stalks, then cook in a little salted water for a few minutes. Chop very finely and cook in a small pan with 1 tablespoon ($\frac{1}{2}$oz) butter and a pinch of salt for a few minutes, then add the meat. Finely chop the *mortadella* and mix in a bowl with the other ingredients and some salt and freshly ground pepper to taste, then use to fill the *agnolotti*. Heat the remaining $\frac{1}{4}$ cup (2oz) butter with the tomatoes (which have been put through a food mill) and a pinch of salt and simmer gently until thick and creamy. Cook the *agnolotti* in plenty of boiling salted water, drain and mix in a deep serving bowl with the tomato sauce and grated parmesan.

Serves 4

Ravioli ripieni di ragù di pesce · RAVIOLI WITH FISH FILLING

¾ cup dried mushrooms
1 whiting (about ¾lb), filleted
2 anchovy fillets or salt-cured
  anchovies
3 tablespoons olive oil
1 medium onion
1 small carrot
1 small stalk celery
1 clove garlic
1 sprig parsley
2 tablespoons concentrated tomato
  paste (purée) 2 tablespoons
salt and pepper
2¾ cups (sifted) flour
3 eggs
¼ cup butter
⅔ cup grated parmesan cheese

Soak the mushrooms in warm water for 20 minutes, then squeeze out the liquid and chop. Wash the whiting fillets and chop the flesh into small pieces. Wash the anchovies and fillet them if necessary, then chop well and cook in the oil, crushing with a fork in the pan to make a smooth sauce. Add the chopped onion, carrot, celery, garlic, parsley and mushrooms and cook over a moderate heat for a few minutes. Dissolve the concentrated tomato paste (purée) in a little warm water, season with salt and freshly ground pepper and simmer to obtain a smooth, thick sauce. Remove from the heat, stir in the whiting, season with salt to taste, return to the heat and cook until the whiting is done.

Make the pasta as in the basic recipe on page 44 with the flour, eggs and a pinch of salt, then stuff with the fish filling and cook in plenty of boiling salted water. Drain and place in a deep serving dish with the melted butter and plenty of grated parmesan.

Serves 4

Ravioli ai filetti di sogliola alla marchigiana · RAVIOLI WITH FILLETS OF SOLE

2¾ cups (sifted) flour
4 eggs
½ cup very fresh *ricotta* cheese
1 cup grated parmesan
grated nutmeg
2 medium sole, filleted
1 small carrot
1 stalk celery
2 cloves garlic
4 tablespoons olive oil
6 tablespoons dry white wine
1lb canned (tinned) peeled tomatoes, pureed
salt and pepper
1 sprig parsley

Make the ravioli according to the basic recipe on page 44. Make the cheese filling in advance. Beat together the *ricotta*, 1 egg, ⅓ cup (1oz) grated parmesan and a pinch of nutmeg and salt to taste. Set aside. Clean the sole and fillet them if this has not been done. Chop the carrot, celery and garlic and fry gently in the oil, then add the fillets of sole and brown on both sides. Raise the heat and add the wine, let it evaporate, then lower the heat and add the puréed tomatoes. Season with salt and freshly ground pepper and simmer covered until done. Shortly before removing the saucepan from the fire, add the chopped parsley.

Stuff the ravioli with the cheese filling, cook in plenty of boiling salted water and serve with the fish sauce so there are two fillets on top of each helping. Serve the remaining grated parmesan separately.

Serves 4

Left: ravioli ai filetti di sogliola alla marchigiana

Ravioli ripieni di pesce e spinaci · RAVIOLI WITH FISH AND SPINACH FILLING

1 medium whiting (about 10oz)
1lb uncooked spinach
2 anchovy fillets or salt-cured anchovies
3 tablespoons olive oil
salt and pepper
2¾ cups (sifted) flour
3 eggs
¼ cup butter

Clean and fillet the fish, then chop in small pieces. Wash the spinach very carefully and cook in very little water, squeeze out the liquid and chop well. Wash the anchovies and fillet if necessary, then chop and cook in the oil, crushing them in the pan with a fork to make a smooth sauce. Add the spinach and cook for a few minutes. Add the minced whiting, season with salt and freshly ground pepper and cook over a moderate heat for 5 or 6 minutes. Remove from the heat and put through a food mill to obtain a thick creamy filling; use this to stuff the ravioli, made as in the basic recipe on page 44. Cook in plenty of boiling salted water, drain and serve with melted butter.

Serves 4

177

Tortelloni verdi gratinati · GREEN TORTELLONI WITH CHEESE FILLING

3 tablespoons olive oil
$\frac{1}{4}$lb ground (minced) lean beef
1 onion
4 large ripe or canned (tinned) peeled
   tomatoes
salt and pepper
$\frac{1}{2}$ cup *ricotta* cheese
1$\frac{3}{4}$ cups grated parmesan cheese
1 pinch nutmeg
2$\frac{3}{4}$ cups (sifted) flour
2 eggs
$\frac{1}{2}$lb uncooked spinach
$\frac{1}{4}$ cup butter
1$\frac{1}{3}$ cups, sliced, very fresh *mozzarella*
   cheese

Make the meat sauce: heat the oil and brown the beef and finely chopped onion. Put the tomatoes through a food mill and add to the sauce. Season with salt and freshly ground pepper and simmer uncovered until smooth and thick. Make the filling for the *tortelloni*: beat together the *ricotta*, half the grated parmesan and nutmeg and salt to taste.

Make a green pasta dough with the flour, eggs and spinach (carefully washed, drained and chopped), as in the basic recipe on page 44, then stuff with the *ricotta* filling. Cook in plenty of boiling salted water, drain and put in an ovenproof dish with the melted butter and rest of the grated parmesan. Cover with finely sliced *mozzarella* and pour over the meat sauce. Bake in a moderate oven for about 15 minutes and serve very hot.

Serves 4

Above: tortelloni verdi gratinati

Rotolo di pasta con spinaci e ricotta · PASTA ROLL WITH SPINACH AND RICOTTA

1lb uncooked spinach
$\frac{1}{3}$ cup butter
3 tablespoons concentrated tomato
   paste (purée)
$\frac{1}{2}$ teaspoon meat extract
1 teaspoon finely chopped onion
salt and pepper
1$\frac{1}{4}$ cups (sifted) flour
1 egg
1 egg yolk
1 cup *ricotta* cheese
$\frac{1}{4}$ cup grated parmesan cheese

Wash the spinach very well and discard the stalks. Cook in very little salted water until just tender, drain and leave to cool, then squeeze out the liquid and chop well. Make a simple tomato sauce: heat $\frac{1}{4}$ cup (2 oz) butter until it foams, then add the concentrated tomato paste (purée) diluted with stock made by dissolving meat extract in $\frac{3}{4}$ cup (6 fl oz) hot water, the chopped onion, salt and a little freshly ground pepper. Let it thicken over a very low heat then put to one side. Mix the flour, 1 whole egg and 1 egg yolk to make a firm, elastic dough and knead until you hear the air bubbles pop when you cut it. Roll out not too thin in a rectangle and place on a lightly floured cloth. Heat the spinach in 2 tablespoons (1oz) butter, season with salt and freshly ground pepper and remove from the heat, then stir in the *ricotta* to make a smooth, soft filling. Spread evenly over the pasta dough leaving an edge about 1in wide uncovered, then use the floured cloth to roll up the pasta, and wrap it carefully in a thin gauze cloth which will stick to the pasta. Tie both ends firmly so it keeps its shape perfectly while cooking. Place the roll in boiling water in a large oval casserole and cook for about 30 minutes, depending on whether you have made a short stubby roll or a long thin one. Carefully remove from the cloth and place on a serving dish, then cut into slices and serve with grated parmesan and the tomato sauce.

For a milder flavour serve with melted butter rather than tomato sauce, and pop the roll into a hot oven for 3–4 minutes before serving.

Serves 4

Below: rotolo di pasta con spinaci e ricotta

RECIPES FROM PAST TIMES AND FOREIGN LANDS

Vermicelli a vongole · VERMICELLI WITH CLAMS

1¾lb clams
5 tablespoons olive oil
salt and pepper
1 sprig parsley
¾lb *vermicelli*

Wash the clams well and cook in a little water over high heat until they open. Remove from their shells and put in a bowl, then filter the cooking liquid through a fine cloth and reserve. Heat the oil in a large pan, stir in the cooking liquid and reduce a little. Season with salt and pepper and add the chopped parsley at the last moment, and then the clams.

Cook the *vermicelli* in plenty of boiling salted water until still quite firm, drain and add to the sauce and stir well so the pasta absorbs all the flavour. Put in a deep bowl and serve immediately.

No grated cheese is necessary with this delicate dish.

Serves 4

Maccheroni incaciati al sugo di pesce · MACARONI WITH FISH SAUCE

4 large ripe or canned (tinned) peeled
  tomatoes
1 onion
4 tablespoons olive oil
2 medium whiting (about 10oz each),
  filleted
3 leaves basil
salt and pepper
1 sprig parsley
$\frac{3}{4}$lb macaroni

Plunge the tomatoes in boiling water remove the skins, cut in half and squeeze out the seeds and liquid, or put canned (tinned) tomatoes through a food mill. Cut the onion into thin slices and cook in the oil until transparent, then add the fish fillets. Sauté for a few minutes, add the tomatoes and basil, season with salt and freshly ground pepper and simmer over a moderate heat until thick, stirring occasionally so the sauce does not burn. Just before removing from the heat add the finely chopped parsley. Cook the macaroni in plenty of boiling salted water, drain while still firm and put in a deep serving bowl with the fish sauce.

Serves 4

Timpano di vermicelli granito · VERMICELLI AU GRATIN WITH FISH SAUCE

$\frac{3}{4}$ cup dried mushrooms
5 tablespoons olive oil
$\frac{1}{2}$ lb flounder, sole, haddock, etc.
salt and pepper
1 sprig parsley, chopped
$\frac{3}{4}$ lb *vermicelli*
3 anchovy fillets or salt-cured
  anchovies
1 small can (tin) *petit pois*
2 tablespoons capers
10 green olives, pitted (stoned)
1 tablespoon butter
4 tablespoons dry breadcrumbs

Soak the mushrooms for 20 minutes in a little warm water. Heat 1 tablespoon oil in a pan and cook the fish with salt and freshly ground pepper, breaking it up with a fork. Simmer the mushrooms in a pan with a little oil, some salt and the chopped parsley, together with a little of the water the mushrooms soaked in which you have previously strained. Remove from the heat when the sauce has thickened.

Cook the *vermicelli* in plenty of boiling salted water, drain while still very firm and finish cooking in a big pan with the remaining oil in which you have crushed the washed and chopped anchovies. Remove from the heat and let cool. Grease an ovenproof dish with half the butter, sprinkle with breadcrumbs and put in half the pasta so it covers the bottom and sides. Fill the centre with some of the mushroom sauce, then with an even layer of fish, peas, capers and pitted (stoned) green olives. Cover with the remaining *vermicelli*, dot with butter and sprinkle with breadcrumbs, then bake in a moderate oven for about 20 minutes, or until golden brown.

Serves 4

Timpano di maccheroni con le melanzane · MACARONI AND EGGPLANT AU GRATIN

6 or 7 eggplants (aubergines)
¾lb ground (minced) lean beef
1 egg
1 tablespoon flour
½ cup butter
1 onion, chopped
6 tablespoons dry red wine
5 ripe or canned (tinned) peeled
   tomatoes, puréed
salt and pepper
3 tablespoons olive oil
¾lb macaroni
⅔ cup grated parmesan cheese

Slice the eggplants (aubergines) lengthwise, sprinkle with salt and leave to drain for a few minutes in a colander weighed down with a plate to remove the excess liquid. Mix half of the ground meat (mince) in a bowl with some salt and the egg, mixing well with a wooden spoon, then make into 8 little balls. Roll in flour and fry in 1 tablespoon (½ oz) butter until brown on all sides, then leave to drain on absorbent kitchen paper. Heat ¼ cup (2 oz) butter and add the chopped onion and the remaining meat. Brown over a good heat, then add the wine and let it evaporate. Lower the heat, add the tomatoes, season with salt and freshly ground pepper and simmer to obtain a thick sauce. Heat the olive oil and fry the slices of eggplant (aubergine) until crisp and brown, then leave to dry on absorbent kitchen paper.

Cook the macaroni in plenty of boiling salted water, drain and put on a flat plate to cool. Grease an ovenproof dish with the remaining butter, and put in a layer of eggplant (aubergine), then put in half the macaroni. Cover with some of the sauce, then the meatballs fairly closely packed together; sprinkle with grated parmesan and cover with the remaining macaroni and sauce. Sprinkle with parmesan, cover with a final layer of eggplant (aubergine) and bake in a moderate oven for about 15 minutes.

Serves 4

Cannelloni al gratin · CANNELLONI AU GRATIN

$3\frac{1}{4}$ cups (sifted) flour
4 eggs
$\frac{1}{4}$lb calf's sweetbreads
$\frac{1}{2}$lb lean veal
4 tablespoons olive oil
1 sprig rosemary
1 small onion, finely chopped
salt and pepper
6 tablespoons dry white wine
2 tablespoons concentrated tomato
   paste (purée)
$\frac{1}{4}$lb fresh pork sausage meat
$\frac{2}{3}$ cup grated parmesan cheese
pinch nutmeg
1 tablespoon breadcrumbs

Make a pasta dough with the flour, 3 eggs and a pinch of salt, then roll out not too thin and cut into rectangles about 4in × 6in. Blanch the sweetbreads and remove the outer membrane, then cut into pieces along with the veal. Heat the oil with the rosemary for a few minutes, then discard the rosemary. Add the finely chopped onion and brown the veal on all sides, then season with salt and freshly ground pepper. Pour over the wine and let it evaporate, uncovered, until it loses its smell. Add the sweetbreads and cook for just a minute, then put everything through a food mill, reserving the juices in the pan. Stir the concentrated tomato paste (purée) dissolved in warm water into the juices in the pan and keep hot. Mix the ground (minced) meat mixture, 1 beaten egg, sausage meat, half the parmesan and a pinch of nutmeg to taste.

Cook the pasta in plenty of boiling salted water and when half cooked remove with a slotted spoon and put in cold water, then lay out to dry on a damp cloth. Put some filling on one end of each rectangle then roll up and press the ends together. Grease an ovenproof dish and put in the *cannelloni*; pour over the sauce, sprinkle with the remaining parmesan mixed with 1 tablespoon breadcrumbs. Bake in a moderate oven until golden.

Serves 4

Above : cannelloni al gratin

Gnocchi alla parigina · GNOCCHI À LA PARISIENNE

$1\frac{1}{4}$ cups milk
$\frac{1}{2}$ cup butter
$1\frac{3}{4}$ cups (sifted) flour
6 egg yolks
$1\frac{2}{3}$ cups grated parmesan cheese
$\frac{1}{3}$ cup heavy (double) cream

Boil the milk with a small piece of butter and gradually stir in the flour. Cook over a moderate heat until firm and remove from the heat when the mixture leaves the sides of the pan. Leave to cool, then beat in the egg yolks and $1\frac{1}{3}$ cups (4 oz) grated parmesan. Form into little *gnocchi* the size of a walnut and cook in boiling salted water. Remove with a slotted spoon as they rise to the surface and arrange on a greased ovenproof dish. Dot with butter and sprinkle with the remaining parmesan, then bake for a few minutes in a hot oven and serve immediately.

In the traditional French recipe the *gnocchi* are covered with a *béchamel* sauce: mix 2 tablespoons flour with $\frac{1}{4}$ cup (2 oz) melted butter, then slowly stir in the milk and cook until thick. Remove from the heat and beat in cream.

Serves 4

Below : gnocchi alla parigina

PIZZA

The various stages in making pizza are illustrated opposite and on the following pages. For four individual pizzas you need:
3 cups (sifted) flour
2 packed level tablespoons fresh yeast (or 2 dry yeast)
6 tablespoons milk
salt

Dissolve the yeast in a little warm water and break up any lumps with a spoon. Put the flour in a mound on the pastry board or working surface, make a well in the centre and pour in the yeast with the milk and a pinch of salt. Knead well to obtain a smooth soft dough, adding more flour or water as necessary. The dough must then be left to rise: this can be a delicate operation as the time needed will depend on the temperature of the warming place. The ideal temperature is about 86°F, with a high level of humidity. To create this essential humidity put the dough in a large bowl, sprinkle with flour and cover with a damp cloth. The dough will rise in three or four hours or less, depending on the temperature; it must be left until it has doubled in bulk. Divide it into four equal parts and knead each part into a ball. Press down each ball with your fingers to make a flat pancake-shaped pizza not more than $\frac{3}{8}$ in thick, with the edges a little higher than the centre so the topping does not spill over. Garnish to taste and bake in a very hot oven on a greased baking sheet or in a Teflon or other non-stick tart pan.

The word *pizza* does not appear in the [offical Italian] dictionary because it is something made out of flour, and because it is a speciality of the Neapolitans and of the very city of Naples itself. If you want to know what a pizza is take a piece of dough, roll it out, then pummel it a bit with the flat of your hands, cover it with anything at all, moisten it with oil or lard, bake it in the oven and eat it.

Such is Sir Emanuele Rocco's description of the second most important Neapolitan speciality after pasta; it is quoted from the anthology *Usi e Costumi di Napoli* by De Bourcard mentioned in an earlier chapter on pasta. The description is still valid even if richer varieties of pizza are now more in demand than the *pizza napoletana verace* (the true Neapolitan pizza) at the little stalls and shops where the pizza dough is still mixed and baked (although electric ovens have replaced the old wood fires). These new hybrid garnishes are christened according to the pizza-maker's fancy — *alla genovese*, *alla pugliese* or suchlike, although, like spaghetti, pizza is still considered to be a Neapolitan speciality, a fact which, according to Emanuele Rocco at least, makes it somewhat less than exclusive.

A few years before De Bourcard began to compile his anthology another writer, also mentioned earlier (the history of pasta and pizza is in many ways similar), Alexandre Dumas *père*, discussed the subject of pizza in his *Grand Dictionnaire de la Cuisine* in a free and easy style that would appeal to the Neapolitans. Dumas had also seen the *lazzari* or street urchins eating pizza as their winter food, while in the summer they lived on watermelon. The creator of d'Artagnan makes one other important observation: "Pizza is a sort of bun like the ones made at Saint-Denis: it is round in shape and made with the same bread dough. It seems simple enough, but on closer inspection it is really very complicated." He goes on to give a few practical gastronomic details: "Pizza is made with oil, bacon, lard, cheese, tomato or small fish. It is the yardstick by which the whole food market is measured; prices rise and fall according to the price of these ingredients and their relative availability." And here Dumas lies by saying that the cheaper pizzas available are one week old. Since time immemorial even the poorest and simplest folk have always eaten pizza fresh from the oven, and even today commercial pizzas, however false and tasteless, are still made the same day, even though they are reheated under a grill. In the 1950 Italian edition of *Grand Dictionnaire de la Cuisine* edited by Gino Doria, there is a note by this great scholar explaining that Dumas was confusing *la pizza oggi a otto*, or pizza eaten on the spot and paid for a week later, with "eight day-old pizza". In fact, G. Marotta describes in his book *Oro di Napoli* how this form of deferred payment was very common in Naples at the time.

Rocco provides the same information as Dumas, although his gastronomic details are more interesting. "The simplest pizzas, known as pizza with oil and garlic, are sprinkled with oil, then salt, then oregano, then finely chopped garlic. Others are covered with grated cheese, pieces of lard and a few basil leaves. The former are often garnished with little fish as well, and the latter with thin slices of mozzarella, or sometimes with slices of ham, tomatoes or clams etc. Sometimes the dough is folded over the ingredients to make 'calzone'."

Two things can be said about all this: both in 1835, when the original edition of the *Grand Dictionnaire* was planned, and about twenty years later, when Rocco contributed his article, tomatoes were not considered an essential ingredient to give an authentic Neapolitan flavour, so that pizza in fact resembled many other types of flat bun or bread *croissants* made exclusively with white flour and eaten anywhere from Saint-Denis to the dukedom of Modena. Secondly, there is no truth in the story that a *pizzaiolo* (pizza-maker) garnished his pizzas with *mozzarella* to please Queen Margherita, wife of Alfonso of Aragon, thus creating *pizza margherita* as we now know it.

Mozzarella and tomatoes apart, it is worth remarking on the fact that pizza is one of those almost spontaneous inventions that followed on the discovery of the phenomenon of leavening that takes place when certain cereals are cooked in a hot oven (most of all wheat flour), a fact particularly appreciated by Mediterranean peoples from the very earliest times.

It is helpful in making pizza to know that, although there are different theories about the ideal thickness and amount of leaven to use, pizza essentially differs from flat buns or bread in the following ways:

— Pizza is made from a simple dough of flour and yeast dissolved in water or milk without any other ingredients such as oil, lard etc. to make it more crumbly.

— It is only garnished on top and no extra ingredients are added to the dough itself, as is the case with the various buns and breads from Emilia and Modena, which sometimes contain ham mixed with the dough itself.

— Pizza is baked at a *very* high temperature (ideally about 750°F), preferably in a wood oven. This applies to Neapolitan pizza, but the Ligurian variety can be easily adapted to an electric domestic oven as it cooks well at 375°F and is therefore possible for any housewife.

Fried *pizzette* are not really pizzas but beignets, or fritters. This means that the Italian pizza zone begins in Sicily with *sfinciuni*, of which there are two types. The ordinary version is a sort of pizza with tomato sauce, breadcrumbs, anchovies, cheese, onions, oil, salt and pepper which is baked in the oven. Again, according to Alberto Denti di Pirajno (*Siciliani a tavola*, Longanesi) there is a more refined version made by families in Palermo, where the old Sicilian traditions live on, called *pizza di San Vito*. It consists of two sheets of dough made with oil and 2 level tablespoons yeast for every 9 cups (2lb) flour, which are then baked in the oven stuffed with a meat sauce and salami, then garnished with cheese and onion with a glass of wine poured over the top. It is thus more like a *calzone*, with a rich filling, than an ordinary pizza topping.

On the mainland of Italy there is the *pitta chicullata*, a circle of dough covered with sliced tomatoes, oil and hot chilli pepper and then baked in the oven. *Pitta* is obviously another name for pizza, but there is a *pitta maniata* which consists of two circles of dough kneaded at length with eggs and fat and then baked with a filling of hard-boiled eggs, *ricotta*, salami and hot pepper, and which is obviously another relation of *calzoni*. There are many local versions of these pizze and *calzoni* in Apulia and in other parts of Italy. Pizza with stewed mussels and seafood are often called *alla tarantina* although this is not a traditional name.

Going much further north, Paolo Monelli wrote a delightfully civilized gastronomic guide to Italy in 1935, called the *Ghiottone Errante* (*The Wandering Gourmet*), in which he describes a certain powerful pizza from Orbetello with onions, anchovies and a strong, distinctive, uncompromising flavour.

"Empty" pizza is a Tuscan speciality, so called because it is just pizza with rosemary (also known as *pan di ramerino* or rosemary bread), but it is still made with a proper pizza dough like other similar versions from Liguria and is thus different from the many salted *focacce* or buns found there. From Recco on the Riviera di Levante comes a famous cheese pizza. It is so crisp and tasty that it has made Manuelina's restaurant famous (certain old Genoans remember how many years ago after a night out in town the whole merry group found themselves at dawn in Recco and woke up Manuelina, while one particularly persuasive member of the group even persuaded her

to cook them a meal). Far rarer now is a pizza or rather a bread made with *sansa di oliva*, or a sort of purée from the olive pressing before the stones themselves are crushed.

Genoa makes its own contribution to the pizza tradition with a type of vegetable pancake or tart which can also be eaten as a snack. Traditionally the first pizza, or *moretum*, to which an anonymous poet of the Virgilian period dedicated a poem, subsequently translated by Leopardi, consisted of a circle of unleavened dough baked in an oven and then covered with raw vegetables, oil and vinegar – in fact a sort of compromise between all these traditional bread/bun recipes. But modern pizza-makers are more inclined to follow the principles for *smorrenbrod* defined by Oscar Davidsen of Copenhagen as a slice of bread topped with absolutely anything that is at all edible), so it is impossible to define the connection between pizza and *torta*. Finally, Liguria has its own speciality, a soft flat white bun sprinkled with oil and coarse salt, then cut in wedges and sold in a little piece of greaseproof paper from the little trolleys that wheel up and down the railway platform during the few minutes your train has stopped there.

However, it is at Oneglia that a truly Mediterranean pizza is made. This is the *pizza all'Andrea*, dedicated apparently to the famous Italian admiral Andrea Doria, who was native to Oneglia. The bread base is soft and rich – the dough includes durum wheat flour and olive oil so it rises very nicely. It has a thick topping similar to many other pizzas: tomatoes, black olives, anchovy fillets, whole cloves of garlic and lots of fried onion. Three kilometres away at Porto Maurizio there is a slightly different pizza called the *sardenea*, which should have a topping of fresh sardines rather than anchovies. The *sardenaria* of Sanremo has less onion and some *machetto*, the anchovy or sardine paste prepared by the local fishermen. Beyond the frontier with France the *pissaladière* from Nice is a relic of the old links between the county of Nice and Liguria. It goes beyond Nice: even very good restaurants in Toulon or Marseilles serve *pissaladière* as an *entrée* with a topping similar to a Ligurian pizza, but with a very thin crispy base more like the original Neapolitan pizza than anything else.

We cannot include detailed recipes in this rapid survey of Italian pizza cookery, but it is worth mentioning that in Provence and in Liguria, and in countries outside France and Italy, pizza is often baked in a large rectangular tin, then cut into squares or rectangles.

A mixture of old and new traditions have made the pizza into a good substantial dish, but the most popular versions are quick and easy to prepare, and generally include tomato and

191

mozzarella. The best-known are:

— *pizza napoletana* (tomato, garlic, oil and oregano);

— *pizza margherita* (tomato, *mozzarella*, garlic oil, oregano and basil to taste);

— *pizza marinara* (tomato, anchovies, capers, olives and, not in the ''classical'' version, but nearly always added, *mozzarella*);

— *pizza quattro stagioni*, or 4 seasons (divided by strips of dough or a dent into four quarters, each with a different topping).

These basic types can be ''crossed'' (*pizza margherita* can contain anchovies; *pizza napoletana* often comes with *mozzarella* etc.) and varied by adding many other things like ham, cheese, mushrooms, seafood, onions, and, rather less acceptable, the Italian vegetables in oil or vinegar (artichokes, mushrooms, capers, sweet peppers, gherkins etc.).

One thing seems certain: pizza for so long the food of the poorest people is becoming today both in the kitchen and in the market place the most popular of snack foods. It is hard to understand why it has become so popular at a time when everyone is eating less bread, since pizza is only bread with a fairly scant topping (a modern sandwich contains a far richer filling). It is not so much because it is a gastronomic treat that there are snack-bars from Montmartre to Soho variously named for something to do with pizza and pasta, but because pizza is a zany, colourful food. To use a formula from an old film, it is just ''bread, love and fantasy'', not the pervasive erotic love of our modern society, but the simple love the pizza-maker puts into his ancient art.

Massimo Alberini

PIZZA ROMANA

For each pizza: 4 tablespoons puréed canned (tinned) peeled tomatoes, $\frac{1}{3}$ cup (2 oz) diced *mozzarella* cheese, 1 pinch oregano, 2 anchovy fillets. Spread on the pizza in the order given, sprinkle with oil and bake in a very hot oven.

Below: pizza romana

PIZZA MARGHERITA

For each pizza: 4 tablespoons puréed canned (tinned) peeled tomatoes, $\frac{1}{3}$ cup (2 oz) diced *mozzarella*, 3 basil leaves (or a pinch of oregano). Spread on the pizza in the order given, sprinkle with oil and bake in a very hot oven.

See pages 186–187: pizza margherita

PIZZA AL PROSCIUTTO

For each pizza: $\frac{1}{2}$ cup (2 oz) cooked ham cut in thin strips, 4 tablespoons puréed canned (tinned) peeled tomatoes, $\frac{1}{3}$ cup (2 oz) diced *mozzarella*. Spread on the pizza in the order given, sprinkle with oil and bake in a hot oven.

CALZONE ALLA RICOTTA

For each *calzone*: $\frac{1}{2}$ cup ($\frac{1}{4}$lb) *ricotta* cheese, 1 thin slice (1oz) *mortadella*, 2 basil leaves, 1 hard-boiled egg. Mix the ingredients and spread over the pizza. Fold over to make a semi-circle and press the edges close together. Bake in a hot oven like a normal pizza.

Above left: calzone alla ricotta

PIZZA QUATTRO STAGIONI

For each pizza: 1 cup (2 oz) sliced mushrooms, cooked for 15 minutes in a little butter, $\frac{1}{2}$ cup (2 oz) cut ham, $\frac{1}{3}$ cup (2 oz) sliced *mozzarella*, 2 or 3 artichokes in vinegar, 7 or 8 black olives, 1 peeled tomato, oil, salt. Cover the pizza with the puréed tomato and sliced *mozzarella*, then arrange the other ingredients on top in four separate sections.

Above right: pizza quattro stagioni

PIZZA PUGLIESE

For each pizza: $\frac{1}{2}$ cup (2 oz) grated *pecorino* cheese, 1 onion, finely chopped, 2 tablespoons olive oil, 2 tablespoons puréed canned (tinned) peeled tomatoes. Mix 1 tablespoon oil with the pizza dough, then knead and make into the usual round pizza. Garnish with very finely chopped onion, the grated *pecorino* cheese, puréed tomatoes and the remaining oil. Bake in a very hot oven.

Below: pizza pugliese

ACKNOWLEDGMENTS

Mondadori archives: 14, 17, 36, 37, 70; Barilla: 49(ar), 140; Tani Capacchione/Luisa Ricciarini: 135, 137(b), 154; L'esperto/Luisa Ricciarini: front cover; Giorgio Lotti: 23(l), 24, 41, 69(al), 98(l); Paola Martini/Luisa Ricciarini: 77(b), 165(a), 166(b), 179(b), 185; Nimatallah/Luisa Ricciarini: 93(a); Photo Nova: 6, 15, 18, 19, 23(r), 30, 31, 33, 35, 39, 44, 45; Pictor: 12–13; Marco Pizzocaro/Luisa Ricciarini: 49(al/b), 51, 53, 56, 57, 59(a/bl), 62, 63, 72, 73, 75(b), 77(a), 78, 87, 89(a), 90, 91, 93(b), 98(r), 99, 101(ar), 102, 104(b), 107(b), 108, 109, 110(a), 115, 117(ar), 119, 121(b), 125, 127, 128, 129, 142, 147(b), 148(b), 168, 169, 170, 171, 175, 176, 181, 182, 183; Mario Rossi/Luisa Ricciarini: 26, 27, 28, 42, 43, 55, 59(br), 61, 65, 67, 69(ar/b), 71, 75(a), 81, 83, 89(b), 95, 96, 97, 101(al/b), 103, 104(a), 107(a), 110(b), 112, 113, 114, 117(al/b), 118, 121 (a), 122, 131, 132, 134, 137(a), 139, 141, 143, 147(a), 148(a), 151, 153, 155, 156, 158, 159, 161, 163, 165(b), 173, 179(a); Fabio Simon/Luisa Ricciarini: 186–187, 189, 190, 191, 193, 195, back cover; Wolfango Soldati: 25, 84; Studio Iantra: 52.

The publishers wish to thank the restaurants *Antica Locanda Mincio* of Borghetto di Valeggio (Verona, Italy) and *Trattoria al sole* of Falzoni di Volta Mantovana (Mantua, Italy) for their collaboration in preparing some of these dishes.